Timeless Wisdom for the New Millennium

Well over two millennia have passed since Sun Tzu wrote *The Art of War*. Although the rate of change has accelerated in each millennium, the timeless wisdom of the strategic rules set forth by Sun Tzu have not changed. Fundamental strategic truths are the same for all times and all generations.

The objective of this book is to make Sun Tzu's simple and timeless strategies useful to managers in the new millennium. Your success in using ideas from this book is my success. My wish is that this new translation and analysis will contribute to your continued success.

Gerald A. Michaelson

Worldwide Praise for *Sun Tzu: The Art of War for Managers*

The new millennium is where East meets West. This book reveals creative applications of Sun Tzu's strategic wisdom in management.

> Frank L. Hung, Chairman
> Harvard Management Services, Inc.
> Taipei, Taiwan

As global competition approaches the intensity of war, Sun Tzu: The Art of War for Managers *is a brilliant companion, linking time-honored military concepts to sound business strategy. Don't go into battle without it.*

> Bill Griffiths, President
> Fluid Systems Division
> United Dominion Industries, USA

Sun Tzu's Art of War *is the definitive work on military strategy. Michaelson's commentary makes* The Art of War for Managers *the definitive work on business strategy.*

> Roger Eriksson
> ABB Business Academy
> Vasteras, Sweden

Translations available in German, Japanese, Korean, and Spanish.

Sun Tzu

THE ART of WAR for MANAGERS

Sun Tzu

THE ART of WAR FOR MANAGERS

50 Strategic Rules

Gerald A. Michaelson

Adams Media Corporation
Avon, Massachusetts

Published by Adams Media, an F+W Publications Company
57 Littlefield Street, Avon, MA 02322. U.S.A.
www.adamsmedia.com

New translation of *The Art of War*
by Pan Jiabin and Liu Ruixiang
with permission from
Military Science Publishing House
Beijing, China

ISBN: 1-58062-459-6

Printed in Canada.

J I H

Library of Congress Cataloging-in-Publication data
available upon request from the publisher.

This publication is designed to provide accurate and authoritative information with
regard to the subject matter covered. It is sold with the understanding that the publisher is not engaged in rendering legal, accounting, or other professional advice. If
legal advice or other expert assistance is required, the services of a competent professional person should be sought.
—From a *Declaration of Principles* jointly adopted by a Committee of the
American Bar Association and a Committee of Publishers and Associations

Many of the designations used by manufacturers and sellers to distinguish their products are claimed as trademarks. Where those designations appear in this book and
Adams Media was aware of a trademark claim, the designations have been printed in
initial capital letters.

This book is available at quantity discounts for bulk purchases.
For information, call 1-800-872-5627.

Dedication

This book is dedicated in loving memory of
Alexander, Emily, Joann, LeRoy, and Phyllis
and with love to the future of
Danny, Jessica, Katie, and Nicholas.

Contents

Part One
New Translation of *The Art of War*
with Manager's Commentary

Part Two
Applying Sun Tzu's Wisdom

Acknowledgments

As always, Steven and Deanne provided ideas while Jan supported my interest in the strange hobby of searching for business applications from military strategy.

With thanks for the world-class performance of Sandy Belcher, a talented and tireless editor who gets everything right.

Jere Calmes, Jeff Cowell, Carl Glass, Trent Price, Townes Osborn, and Steve Rivkin gave awesome advice concerning major changes in format and content.

My thanks to many friends who offered ideas and input during the eight years of intermittent writing and rewriting of this book. The most recent helpful contributions were offered by Roger Bean, Tim Carpenter, Suzzane Dupes, Tom Gordon, Frank Hung, Erny James, Ed Miles, Irving Mills, Vergil Metts, Allen Pannell, John Shamley, Chuck Sawyer, and Jerry Sentell. My apologies to those I may have missed.

Thanks to friends in Beijing: Zhai Zhihai who introduced me to the new translation, Mr. Chen Yingming for his gracious assistance in arranging contacts, and Ms. Wu Ying for making arrangements with Mr. Chen Shufang, who gave approval on behalf of his publishing house to use this translation of *The Art of War*.

The Lesson of the Concubines

The following story is considered to be of dubious authenticity and not part of the 13 chapters. Some translators include it within their books; others ignore its existence. All narratives are quite similar. You may find interesting lessons in the following version.

Sun Tzu's book, *The Art of War,* earned him an audience with the King of Wu, who said, "I have thoroughly read your 13 chapters. May I submit your theory of managing soldiers to a small test?"

Sun Tzu replied, "Sir, you may."

The King of Wu asked, "Can the test be applied to women?"

Sun Tzu replied that it could, so arrangements were made to bring 180 beautiful women from the palace. Sun Tzu divided them into two companies with one of the King's favorite concubines at the head of each. He then made all of them take spears in their hands and spoke to them: "I presume you know the difference between front and back, right hand, and left hand?"

The women replied, "Yes."

Sun Tzu continued, "When to the sound of drums I order 'eyes front,' look straight ahead. When I order 'left turn,' face toward your left hand. When I order 'right turn,' face toward your right hand. When I order 'about turn,' face around to the back."

After the words of command had been explained, the women agreed they understood. He gave them spears so he could begin the drill. To the sound of drums, Sun Tzu ordered 'right turn.' In response, the women burst out in laughter.

With great patience, Sun Tzu said, "If the instructions and words of command are not clear and distinct, if orders are not thoroughly understood, then the general is to blame." He then repeated the explanations several times. This time he ordered the drums to signal 'left turn,' and again the women burst into laughter.

Then Sun Tzu said, "If the instructions and words of command are not clear and distinct, if orders are not thoroughly understood, the general is to blame. But if commands are clear and the soldiers disobey, then it is the fault of the officers." He immediately ordered the women who were at the head of the two companies to be beheaded.

Of course, the King was watching from a raised pavilion, and when he saw that his two favorite concubines were about to be executed, he was alarmed and swiftly sent down a message: "We are now quite satisfied as to the general's ability to manage troops. Without these concubines, my food and drink will not taste good. It is the King's wish that they not be beheaded."

Sun Tzu replied, "Having received the sovereign's commission to take charge and direct these troops, there are certain orders I cannot accept." He immediately had the two concubines beheaded as an example and appointed the two next in line as the new leaders.

Now the drums were sounded again and the drill began. The women performed all the maneuvers exactly as commanded, turning to the right or left, marching ahead, turning around, kneeling, or rising. They drilled perfectly in precision and did not utter a single sound.

Sun Tzu sent a messenger to the King of Wu saying, "Your Majesty, the soldiers are now correctly drilled and perfectly disciplined. They are ready for your inspection. Put them to any use you desire. As sovereign, you may choose to require them to go through fire and water and they will not disobey."

The King responded, "Our commander should cease the drill and return to his camp. We do not wish to come down and inspect the troops."

With great calm, Sun Tzu said, "This king is only fond of words and cannot carry them into deeds."

Commentary following the story indicates that the King relented, recognized Sun Tzu's ability, and appointed him a general; and Sun Tzu won many battles. In contrast, some historians believe Sun Tzu simply served as a civilian strategist, and others deny his existence, claiming he was actually someone else.

The moral of the story could be a lesson on training, discipline, command structure, role playing, or perhaps job interviews. The thoughtful reader may use his or her imagination to determine applicable lessons.

Introduction

As I stood in the Great Hall of the People in Beijing, China, an entourage was approaching. The next thing I knew I was shaking hands with the Premier of China—Li Peng. The personal introduction was part of a journey to China to present applications of Sun Tzu's strategies for business at an international symposium on *The Art of War*.

Sun Tzu was a practical philosopher who wrote the 7,000-word *The Art of War* in about 500 B.C. I read it while researching my book *Winning the Marketing War* and found the content quite useful.

If you've read James Clavell's *Noble House* or seen the movie *Wall Street*, you've encountered some of the wisdom of this ancient Chinese strategist. In both the book and the movie, major characters quote from Sun Tzu as a foundation for their strategy.

The Art of War might be one of the oldest books you will ever read. Originally written on bamboo strips, this acclaimed work has achieved international recognition as *the* concentrated essence of winning strategy.

For centuries, *The Art of War* has held a preeminent position among both Chinese and Japanese strategists. Many of the sayings of Chairman Mao are simple restatements of Sun Tzu's philosophies.

When Chiang Kai-shek's military attaché advised British military strategist B. H. Liddell Hart that Chinese officers were trained from Hart's books, he replied it was time they went back to Sun Tzu:

> Since in that one short book was embodied almost as much about the fundamentals of strategy and tactics as I [Hart] had covered in more than twenty books. In brief, Sun Tzu was the best short introduction to the study of warfare.

Confirming again that *The Art of War* is *the* sound fundamental text on strategy.

Eastern Versus Western Strategy

The Art of War is the foundation of Eastern strategy. Sun Tzu's central thesis is that you can avoid fighting when you plan the right strategy before the battle.

On War by Carl von Clausewitz, a German officer who wrote in Napoleon's time, is the foundation of much of Western strategy. Clausewitzian theory concentrates on the big battle as the way to win.

Readers will find *On War* filled with convoluted sentences and difficult to read. One English translation is over 600 pages long. Clausewitz's work expresses so many ideas that it can be used to justify any position.

In contrast, *The Art of War* is a masterpiece of simplicity. When comparing Clausewitz and Sun Tzu, strategist Liddell Hart comments: "Sun Tzu has clearer vision, more profound insight, and eternal freshness."

Although there is evidence that a translation of *The Art of War* could have been available to Napoleon, Sun Tzu's work has not generally been considered a contributor to Western military strategy.

Locked within Sun Tzu are secrets for business and personal success. Continued study and analysis of Sun Tzu yields new insights to unlock winning concepts.

A Strategic Manual for Business Leaders

Using Sun Tzu's strategies in business is nothing new. The existence of over one hundred Japanese translations of *The Art of War* indicates it has served as a source of strategic thinking for many Japanese managers. In contrast, only a handful of English translations exist, but they are circulated throughout the business world.

There is much evidence that *The Art of War* is making significant contributions to the thinking of contemporary business leaders. Harvard Professor Michael Porter quoted from Sun Tzu when he lectured the National Football League owners on how they could defeat the now-defunct United States Football League. Venture capitalist Asher Edelman made *The Art of War* required reading for admission to his course on entrepreneuring at Columbia University. Quantity orders for *The Art of*

War have been placed by business organizations, trade unions, and law enforcement agencies. Although Western officers who laid plans for the Gulf War were well versed in Sun Tzu, it would seem as though Saddam Hussein was not.

The Art of War is a classic not only of strategy but also of simplicity. There was nothing very complex about warfare in Sun Tzu's time. It involved land battles of large bodies of troops armed with personal weapons. And the very simplicity of *The Art of War* makes Sun Tzu's lessons readily transferable to business strategy. The ancient principles of Sun Tzu establish a firm foundation for understanding the strategic rules of business in the new millennium.

The lessons of Sun Tzu are thousands of years old, and it is the test of time that makes them valuable to the business manager. Many business lessons have existed for such a short time that they have yet to crystallize as valid strategies. Evidence of respect for the passage of time to give veracity to lessons comes from a Chinese historian who was asked in 1925 to identify the lessons of the French Revolution. He replied, "I would love to, but it is still too early to tell."

Strategy and Tactics

The fundamental principles of strategy are the same for all managers, all times, and all situations. Only the tactics change—and tactics are modified to the times.

Strategy is best defined as "doing the right thing," while tactics is "doing things right." Where does strategy end and tactics begin? Admiral Mahan in his work on sea power said, "Contact is a word which perhaps better than any other indicates the dividing line between tactics and strategy."

Strategy stops at the border in war and at the headquarters door in business; tactics begins with contact with the customer.

Sun Tzu's *The Art of War* provides fundamental lessons for contemporary strategic thought and serves as a fertile source of ideas for tactics.

About This Edition

Because there are so few English language translations of *The Art of War*, the emergence of a new translation has special significance. I felt fortunate indeed when I received this translation in Beijing at a symposium sponsored by "The Research Society of Sun Tzu's *The Art of War*." Translation of Chinese ideograms into English is a complex task because each character can have many different meanings. Consequently, the personal and professional backgrounds of the translators tend to determine the wording of the translation. The Chinese language scholars who undertook the difficult task of translating from the original documents concentrated on finding the most accurate interpretations of the ideograms.

As author, I made an exhaustive search to locate all English language translations. Each translation has been reviewed to find areas where different interpretations would benefit the reader. These differing interpretations can be found throughout the text.

Eastern and Western strategic writings exist as two distinct and separate sources of information, seldom communicating with each other. Western strategists build upon the strengths of previous Western strategists; Eastern strategists similarly reinforce each other. Neither builds on the strength of the other. An important contribution of this work is to provide a conceptual linkage between the fundamental lessons of the two. By analyzing key concepts from both Eastern and Western strategic thought, you gain an insight into how *both* can strengthen your strategy *and* tactics.

This book does not propose a short list of key strategies, but rather is formulated around the understanding that strategy is a mental process. The best strategy comes from the right mindset. Clausewitz said, "Theory can give no formula with which to solve problems. It lets the mind take a look at objects and their relations and then the mind goes to higher regions of action, there to act." *Sun Tzu: The Art of War for Managers* provides a refreshing way to immerse oneself in the great strategic thinking which nurtures the mind.

This new translation of Sun Tzu is a joy to read—and read again. Sun Tzu's lessons can be applied to real-life situations and serve as an everyday resource for all kinds of strategic thought. For example, one version of *The Art of War* relates Sun Tzu's principles to winning in the stock market. An English translation, *The Art of Strategy*, is organized as a template for the strategies of life.

The strategic lessons in *The Art of War* have become a general construct to solve a variety of problems. Although the original text is founded in military strategy, the applications in this book focus on strategic issues for managers.

Reader's Guide

Like the original work, Part One is divided into 13 chapters. Unlike the original work, each chapter is subdivided into three to six discrete strategic rules.

Each chapter has the same title as the original translation. The first page lists the strategic rules in that chapter followed by a brief commentary.

Because the flow of the book faithfully maintains the sequential order of Sun Tzu's translation, there is no modern strategic construct. Rather, each strategic rule stands alone as an idea generator for the contemporary strategist.

A useful guide to practical applications of Sun Tzu's wisdom is presented in Part Two where successful managers discuss their experiences. Part Two also includes an outline of Sun Tzu's key concepts to aid in application.

Because the content of the book flows from Sun Tzu's philosophy, it should not be considered as a complete modern strategic manual. Instead, the value of this book is its ability to simplify the complexity of strategic thinking. While you may want to take the strategic wisdom of Sun Tzu seriously, do not take the modern translation of the ancient words too literally.

Gerald A. Michaelson

Part One

New Translation of

The Art of War

with Manager's Commentary

Reflecting on Sun Tzu's work is to the business manager
what weight lifting is to the champion athlete
—an exercise that makes one stronger.

John Kohut
Beijing Bureau Chief
South China Post

1

Laying Plans

Strategic Rules
Thoroughly Assess Conditions
Compare Attributes
Look for Strategic Turns

The vision of what the organization wants to be must be planned with an awareness of reality. That is why this chapter focuses on assessment.

The vision components articulate purpose, mission, guiding values, and a vivid image of the organization's future. From the vision, leaders can determine the strategy, set strategic initiatives, and align the organization.

The more sophisticated the planning process becomes, the harder it is to introduce the flexibility that accommodates changes in the situation. In rigid systems, planning and obedience to the plan are regarded as the key to victory. Carefully laid plans rigorously implemented without deviation are regarded as *the way* to overcome the inevitable confusion. As ever-increasing time and attention are focused on "the process of planning," the successful execution of the plan becomes secondary. However, any football coach can tell you that rigidity does not win games. Every coach has plans that allow for flexibility in formations to adapt to reality. It follows that it is not strategists who cause changes in the plan—it is reality.

A common mistake is to consider planning as only a mental process, an idea in our head that simply looks at the past and adjusts for the future. If your plan is not in writing, you do not have a plan at all. Instead, you have only a dream, a vision, or perhaps even a nightmare. The simple written plan works best.

Thoroughly Assess Conditions—Translation

Sun Tzu says:

War is a matter of vital importance to the state; a matter of life and death, the road either to survival or to ruin. Hence, it is imperative that it be thoroughly studied.

Therefore, to make assessment of the outcome of a war, one must compare the various conditions of the antagonistic sides in terms of the *five constant factors:**

1. moral influence
2. weather
3. terrain
4. commander
5. doctrine

These five constant factors should be familiar to every general. He who masters them wins; he who does not is defeated.

*Business Parallels to the Five Constant Factors

1. **Moral influence means a "spirit of mission."** The strength of belief that the purpose is morally sound rallies a fighting spirit and generates a firestorm of commitment.
2. **Weather equates to "outside forces."** The surge of consolidation that is sweeping through every industry is an outside force, as is the emergence of world competition, and the influence of environmentalism.
3. **Terrain is the "marketplace."** As the general must know the terrain, so the strategy must consider the scene of action—people, place, product, promotion, price, etc.
4. **Commander has an equivalent in "leadership."** The names keep changing, but the principles of leadership remain the same.
5. **Doctrine is comparable to "guiding principles."** Understand and apply the fundamental principles that determine success.

Thoroughly Assess Conditions—Manager's Commentary

Good assessment is the foundation of a successful operation.

When the management of a major pharmaceutical company found that product development activity was decreasing, an assessment revealed the reason. Although senior managers claimed development was a team effort, analysis of their 25 most profitable drugs revealed that two people initiated 10 of them. The reason product development declined was because both people had moved to positions where they were no longer in the development stream.[1]

Every assessment must include a thorough analysis of how to increase business with existing customers. As proof, an Ogilvy & Mather analysis showed that the return on the marketing investment to existing customers can be many times greater than to prospective customers. The greatest source of increased sales and profits is from those who know you and are now purchasing your products.

In today's business world, the assessment before the plan is often ignored in the rush to action. When action is taken without a thorough assessment of the situation, too often people begin working on the wrong things. In these circumstances, the result will be that a lot of effort is expended with no gain.

Assessments are simply methodologies for gathering data in a structured process designed to elicit facts or perceptions. Assessments can be internal or external. They can be conducted by one or more individuals. Assessments can be surveys distributed to everyone or interviews conducted across a vertical slice of the organization.

Good assessments go beyond the current situation. They dig into underlying causes and search for new and better ways to achieve success. To achieve good results, ask questions in pairs so that the first question determines the perception of the current status, while the second reveals opportunities. For example, the first question might ask for a definition of an objective, while the second would ask for ideas about how the objective should be achieved.

When assessments are conducted by an external organization, respondents usually feel they have a better chance of giving anonymous input.

This provides the opportunity for gathering more accurate data. Clearly define the problem before seeking a solution. Do not limit your planning horizon to what can be accomplished with existing tools. If the only tool you have is a hammer, everything will look like a nail.

Internally, the assessment provides information on strengths and weaknesses that can energize and direct self-renewal. Externally, the assessment reveals threats and opportunities.

Compare Attributes—Translation

Sun Tzu continues:

Therefore, to forecast the outcome of a war *the attributes of the antagonistic sides should be analyzed** by making the following seven comparisons:

1. Which sovereign possesses greater moral influence?
2. Which commander is more capable?
3. Which side holds more favorable conditions in weather and terrain?
4. On which side are decrees better implemented?
5. Which side is superior in arms?
6. On which side are officers and men better trained?
7. Which side is stricter and more impartial in meting out rewards and punishments?

By means of these seven elements, I can forecast victory or defeat.

If the sovereign heeds these stratagems of mine and acts upon them, he will surely win the war, and I shall, therefore, stay with him. If the sovereign neither heeds nor acts upon them, he will certainly suffer defeat, and I shall leave.

*We must compare ourselves with our foe.

A. L. Sadler

A Strategic Moral

Following the success of the Prussian Army in the Franco-Prussian War, the British General Staff sent a team of aristocrats to find out the secret of success. They reported the Prussian troops were all clean shaven with short cropped hair. The British Army copied this. It remains a law to this day.

The moral of the story is: Don't copy the wrong thing! (Or don't send aristocrats to do competitive studies.)

Compare Attributes—Manager's Commentary

Compare competitive strengths and weaknesses.

When Coke and Pepsi engage in competitive battles, or when P&G determines how to increase market share, these organizations use competitive marketing research as an input ingredient. When Xerox determined it wanted to be a world-class competitor, it benchmarked every process to determine how to make that process the best in its class.

Comparisons of attributes can be made in several ways: either a direct competitive comparison of strengths and weaknesses or benchmarking that studies comparable processes in any other organization. Benchmarking is a learning experience that "steals shamelessly" from friend and foe alike.

When Ford benchmarked six other well-run companies, it found the following key attributes: executives spent time outside their offices communicating with employees, people and their skills were a competitive advantage, trust replaced controls, cross-functional teams developed cutting-edge products and services, bureaucracy was out and teams were in, authority was delegated, training was readily available, and each benchmarked company said it was customer driven.

At IBM Rochester, computer manufacturing cycle time extended over a period of 246 days from ordering parts to shipping. Through benchmarking, the cycle time was reduced to less than 30 days.

As people on a benchmarking team observe successful new practices elsewhere, they become enthusiastic champions of change. For example, when an international electronics company benchmarked its plants by function, benchmarking teams found several plants had extremely efficient manufacturing processes. The people involved in the benchmarking activity championed the rapid acceptance of the more efficient processes throughout the organization.

A Fortune 500 company benchmarked attributes other large organizations considered key to success. The best companies listed processes that achieved results as the keys to success while less successful ones ignored the process and simply listed the results—as though each was unaware of the fact that process performance determines results.

A technique called "bench racing" offers an opportunity to visualize your journey through obstacles to a successful finish. The idea comes from runners "sitting on the bench" and imagining themselves racing around the track outrunning competitors.[2]

Look for Strategic Turns—Translation

Sun Tzu continues:

Having paid attention to the advantages of my stratagems, *the commander must create a helpful situation over and beyond the ordinary rules.** By "situation" I mean he should act expediently in accordance with what is advantageous in the field and so meet any exigency.

All warfare is based on deception. Therefore, when able to attack, we must pretend to be unable; when employing our forces, we must seem inactive; when we are near, we must make the enemy believe we are far away; when far away, we must make him believe we are near.

Offer a bait to allure the enemy, when he covets small advantages; strike the enemy when he is in disorder. If he is well prepared with substantial strength, take double precautions against him. If he is powerful in action, evade him. If he is angry, seek to discourage him. If he appears humble, make him arrogant. If his forces have taken a good rest, wear them down. If his forces are united, divide them.

Launch the attack where he is unprepared; take action when it is unexpected.

These are the keys to victory for a strategist. However, it is impossible to formulate them in detail beforehand.

Now, the commander who gets many scores during the calculations in the temple* before the war will have more likelihood of winning. The commander who gets few scores during the calculations in the temple before the war will have less chance of success. With many scores, one can win; with few scores, one cannot. How much less chance of victory has one who gets no scores at all! By examining the situation through these aspects, I can foresee who is likely to win or lose.

*The leader's responsibility in planning is explained in another translation:

. . . the general must create situations which will contribute to accomplishment of plans.
General Tao Hanzhang

Look for Strategic Turns—Manager's Commentary

Develop strategies that go beyond conventional rules.

When the minutemen faced the redcoats on the open battlefield of Concord in the traditional frontal confrontation of the time, the minutemen lost. Then, the minutemen made a fundamental shift in their battle tactics and fired on the redcoats from behind stone fences as they returned to Boston. This shift in tactics initiated a strategic turn in combat as the new strategy of skirmishing contributed to the success of the American Revolution.

Externally Focused Strategic Turns: Wal-Mart's initial strategy focused on small towns. Wherever it invaded, competitive merchandising strategy was changed forever. The advent of mass-merchants like Wal-Mart at one extreme of retailing and specialty boutiques at the other reshaped merchandising strategies across a wide variety of industries.

ESPN is an example of a cable network that heralded a new strategy in marketing. ESPN doesn't have viewers; it has fans that make it a competitive powerhouse. Originally a network with a lot of sporting events, ESPN has reshaped itself into a network for sports junkies. It supplies sporting news and events to every single continent including Antarctica.[3]

Internally Focused Strategic Turns: At the Tactical Air Command during six and one-half years of General Bill Creech's leadership, dramatic improvements in combat readiness were made with no additional people or money. To achieve this awesome record, Creech changed the internal operating strategy to focus on decentralization of authority. His commanders immersed themselves periodically in operations—for example, spending a week with a night maintenance crew. Throughout his command, he applied the principles of quality management as outlined in his best selling book *The Five Pillars of TQM* (product, process, organization, leadership, and commitment).[4]

As a result, the combat capability of the Tactical Air Command doubled and billions of dollars were saved. Out-for-maintenance aircraft were reduced 71 percent, and monthly sorties increased 80 percent (the productivity bottom line). Fighter parts delivery time was reduced dramatically, and aircraft accident safety increased 275 percent.

At Monsanto, the internal strategic turn was to transform a commodity chemical company into a genetic engineering firm.

2

Waging War

Strategic Rules
Marshal Adequate Resources
Make Time Your Ally
Everyone Must Profit from Victories
Know Your Craft

Since the ideal strategy is whatever works best, it follows that implementation is a powerful component of the strategic rollout. The tactical implementation plan is as important as the strategic plan because it takes the vision and strategy to the point of contact.

A European strategist, Captain Johnstone, wrote in 1916:

> You do not know how the enemy is disposed? Fight and find out.
> The decisive attack can only be confidently fixed after some fighting.
> The tentative attack is not a separate fight, but the beginning of the
> battle. Launch a formation against the whole front and you learn the
> shape.[1]

With the right strategy, the battle is only half won; the strategy succeeds only with professional execution of tactics. Problems arise when planning is separated from execution. This is like separating thinking from doing and diffuses responsibility.

The important thing is to get started. Too much time spent in planning can breed indecisiveness and error. It is often better to engage in some form of simultaneous planning and implementation. This can be as difficult as changing a tire while the car is moving. Tactical plans must be shaped in relation to reality with the information learned from contact.

In every endeavor, the abnormal is normal and uncertainty is certain. A contingency plan should be prepared to allow for the abnormal. The exercise of preparing the contingency plan yields insights into threats and opportunities.

Close examination of companies with great reputations for long-range planning reveals they also focus on short-term gains. That is, they play for the championship one day at a time with a consistent focus on long-range direction.

Marshal Adequate Resources—Translation

Sun Tzu says:

Generally, operations of war involve one thousand swift chariots, one thousand heavy chariots and one hundred thousand mailed troops with the transportation of provisions for them over a thousand li. Thus the expenditure at home and in the field, the stipends for the entertainment of state guests and diplomatic envoys, the cost of materials such as glue and lacquer and the expense for care and maintenance of chariots and armour, will amount to one thousand pieces of gold a day. *An army of one-hundred-thousand men can be raised only when this money is in hand.**

*The point that funds must be available before the attack is launched is emphasized in another translation:

Only when you have in hand one thousand pieces of gold for each day can the hundred thousand troops be mobilized.

Roger Ames

Although many translators refer to the required funds as pieces of gold, the Chinese did not have gold coins in Sun Tzu's time. The money was probably ounces of silver.

Marshal Adequate Resources—Manager's Commentary

Invest adequate resources so the operation can be sustained.

Home Depot, Toys 'Я' Us, and other giant category killers in the retailing marketplace understand how to marshal enough resources to overwhelm the market. By combining the concentration of an overwhelming assortment of merchandise with the propaganda of everyday low prices, they suck up market share like crazy.

Why is it that the cry from every business failure is: "We ran out of money." Of course they did! But the real problem was probably one or more of the following: not enough managerial talent or operational skill, wrong products or services, or one of a myriad of other inadequate resources required to make the organization successful.

The failure of many airline start-ups is an obvious business parallel to Sun Tzu's expressed need to have enough resources to survive. Often, these business failures are accompanied by an announcement that the organization ran out of capital before it could generate enough business to be profitable. So it is that all business problems eventually become financial problems.

In every battle, the one with the most resources has the odds in his favor. As Damon Runyon said, "The battle may not go to the strong, or the race to the swift, but that's the way to bet."

The problem of adequate resources is especially critical in start-ups because they do not have the base of loyal customers that sustains mature businesses in an economic downturn.

Allocation of adequate resources for development of future products and services assures success. In its first full year as an independent company, Lucent Technologies invested 11 percent of revenues in its Bell Research center, which secures an average of three new patents every day. SmithKline Beecham and Microsoft invest more than 15 percent of sales in research and development.[2]

To achieve success, you must have superiority. However, that superiority is always relative. It is only necessary to answer the question: What is the allowable limit of resources to allocate? If you are truly determined to win, there is no upper limit. However, this does not mean you should recklessly squander resources. When resources are depleted and cannot be replenished, the result will be bankruptcy.

Make Time Your Ally—Translation

Sun Tzu continues:

In directing such an enormous army, a speedy victory is the main object.

If the war is long delayed, the men's weapons will be blunted and their ardor will be dampened. If the army attacks cities, their strength will be exhausted. Again, if the army engages in protracted campaigns, the resources of the state will not suffice. Now, when your weapons are blunted, your ardor dampened, your strength exhausted and your treasure spent, neighboring rulers will take advantage of your distress to act. In this case, no man, however wise, is able to avert the disastrous consequences that ensue.

*Thus, while we have heard of stupid haste in war, we have not yet seen a clever operation that was prolonged.** There has never been a case in which a prolonged war has benefited a country. Therefore, only those who understand the dangers inherent in employing troops know how to conduct war in the most profitable way.

Hence, what is valued in war is a quick victory, not prolonged operations.

*Crude yet quick strategies have been known. But skill has yet to be observed in prolonged operations.

R. L. Wing

Speed Wins

Throughout history, winning generals developed disciplines and systems for moving faster than their opponents. Napoleon's troops marched at 120 paces per minute while his opponents marched at 70 paces. Since Napoleon's troops marched almost twice as fast as his opponents, speed alone gave him a tremendous advantage that was a major contributor to his success.

Sun Tzu's point is not that speed can overcome stupidity. Operations must be completed rapidly because when actions take too long, the chance increases for errors and unforeseen events to contribute to failure.

Make Time Your Ally—Manager's Commentary

The key is to become rapidly effective and efficient.

Cisco, Compaq, and Dell are examples of fast moving companies that won positions in PCs and computer networking. Internally, cycle time reduction and just-in-time systems have increased the effectiveness and efficiency of production.

A speedy victory is indeed the main objective, and the value of time—being a little ahead of your opponent—has contributed to many victories. Achieving this advantage involves both getting started quickly and rapidly attaining a position of strength.

Building strength rapidly is, in itself, a clever advantage either because you take the opponent unaware or because the swift concentration of multiple elements creates the force of simultaneous action. So it is that the first one to the river usually crosses without difficulty.

The speed with which a position is occupied is critical. Those who own a position early may need to expend less resources defending it than those who come later and must try to occupy that position. The defense of an occupied position is always less costly than the expenditure required to take that position.

Because the high cost of acquiring new customers depletes financial resources more rapidly than the cost of keeping existing customers, new business ventures must move rapidly to build a loyal customer base.

Here are a few key issues in making time an ally:

- As a rule, earliest is best. Time saved is time gained.
- The later you start, the more you require.
- The more urgent the need for a decision, the longer it takes.
- Rapid decision making produces rapid execution.
- Rapid action is simultaneous action.
- Delayed decisions inevitably lose their positive quality.
- All the positive consequences of speed accrue to the early offensive.

- The less you delay:
  - the less apt you are to be surprised.
  - the less ready will be your competitor.
  - the greater the probability your time of attack will be earlier than expected.

As a result, your opponent will be surprised and the consequences will accrue in your favor.[3]

Everyone Must Profit from Victories—Translation

Sun Tzu continues:

Those adept in employing troops do not require a second levy of conscripts or more than two provisionings. They carry military supplies from the homeland and make up for their provisions relying on the enemy. Thus the army will be always plentifully provided.

When a country is impoverished by military operations, it is because an army far from its homeland needs a distant transportation. Being forced to carry supplies for great distances renders the people destitute. On the other hand, the local price of commodities normally rises high in the area near the military camps. The rising prices cause financial resources to be drained away. When the resources are exhausted, the peasantry will be afflicted with urgent exactions. With this depletion of strength and exhaustion of wealth, every household in the homeland is left empty. Seven-tenths of the people's income is dissipated and six-tenths of the government's revenue is paid for broken-down chariots, worn-out horses, armour and helmets, arrows and crossbows, halberds and bucklers, spears and body shields, draught oxen and heavy wagons.

Hence, a wise general is sure of getting provisions from the enemy countries. One zhong of grains obtained from the local area is equal to twenty zhong shipped from the home country; one dan of fodder in the conquered area is equal to twenty dan from the domestic store.

Now in order to kill the enemy, our men must be roused to anger; to gain the enemy's property, our men must be rewarded with war trophies. Accordingly, in chariot battle, when more than ten chariots have been captured, those who took the enemy chariot first should be rewarded. Then, the enemy's flags and banners should be replaced with ours; the captured chariots mixed with ours and mounted by our men. The prisoners of war should be kindly treated and kept. This is called "becoming stronger in the course of defeating the enemy."

Everyone Must Profit from Victories—Manager's Commentary

Strengthen human resources and material assets with each victory.

When a rival in mergers and acquisitions reduced bonuses, Merrill Lynch swooped in with job offers. Said one defector, "I figured Merrill Lynch would always pay me when I had a good year." This employee believed that with the change in jobs would come a direct connection between victory and personal gain.[4]

While I was visiting the national headquarters of one of America's most successful companies, one of its major competitors announced it was going out of business. Within minutes, you could hear secretaries on the phone advising branch managers to immediately interview and hire the best of the now-defunct competitor's salespeople (who would also have contacts with the best prospects). As Sun Tzu says, "This is called 'becoming stronger in the course of defeating the enemy.'" What a loss of good fortune it would be to win the battle and not become stronger.

Too often, a corporate acquisition results in a "housecleaning" of very competent and experienced people. The people who are terminated in the interest of financial efficiencies are often those who really know the customers, the culture, and the subtle elements necessary for success. Because these experienced people are terminated, the acquired company becomes weaker before it becomes stronger, if it survives at all.

The acquisition strategy of many successful companies has been to keep the original owners and staff of acquired companies as active managers while providing the financial resources to power future growth. The chairman of a successful business built on friendly acquisitions said, "One of the key objectives in an acquisition is to retain the existing management. They are the people who built the business, and if we are going to buy that business, it is important to utilize their strengths."

The opportunity to profit from victories also applies to internal recognition and reward programs. Think about providing opportunities for everyone to win. Make the award cycle short and issue rewards immediately after the event. Always gather an audience when you give recognition.

Know Your Craft—Translation

Sun Tzu continues:
And therefore the general who understands war is the controller of his people's fate and the guarantor of the security of the nation.

Qualities of Leadership

Thousands of years ago, one of Sun Tzu's commentators, Ho Yen-hsi, wrote, "The difficulties in the appointment of a commander are the same today as they were in ancient times"[5]—and that was said during what we consider ancient times.

Napoleon in his maxims said, "It is exceptional and difficult to find in one man all the qualities necessary for a great general. That which is most desirable, and which instantly sets a man apart, is that his intelligence or talent are balanced by his character or courage. If his courage is the greater, the general heedlessly undertakes things beyond his ability. If, on the contrary, his character or courage is less than his intelligence, he does not dare carry out his plans."

Mao Tse-tung wrote, "In actual life we cannot ask for an invincible general; there have been few such generals since ancient times. We ask for a general who is both brave and wise; who usually wins battles in the course of war—a general who combines wisdom with courage."

British Major General J. F. C. Fuller writes about a competitive quality: "Originality, not conventionality, is one of the main pillars of generalship. To do something that the enemy does not expect, is not prepared for, something which will surprise him and disarm him morally. To be always thinking ahead and to be always peeping round corners. To spy out the soul of one's adversary, and to act in a manner which will astonish and bewilder him, this is generalship."

Military writers also agree that an important quality of an ideal leader is a concern for people. In *On the Psychology of Military Incompetence*, Dixon points out that humanitarianism is a prerequisite for high morale and physical health.

Know Your Craft—Manager's Commentary

Master the expertise required to win.

When *Fortune* magazine listed the 10 most admired companies, it recognized the leadership of each:

1. General Electric: Jack Welch
2. Coca-Cola: Douglas Ivester
3. Microsoft: Bill Gates
4. Dell Computer: Michael Dell
5. Berkshire Hathaway: Warren Buffett
6. Wal-Mart: David Glass
7. Southwest Airlines: Herb Kelleher
8. Intel: Craig Barrett
9. Merck: Raymond Gilmarten
10. Walt Disney: Michael Eisner[6]

In each case, the leaders of these companies have profound industry knowledge and most have grown with the organization. Many star executives are long-term experts in their craft.

When the early Romans built an aqueduct, the engineer who designed the structure stood under it when the scaffolding was removed. His expertise in his craft truly determined whether he lived or died.

Computer people should run computer companies (witness the disastrous, short term of John Scully when he moved from Pepsi to Apple), beverage people should run beverage companies, and airline people should run airline companies. The credentials of an industry expert are impressive. Who would argue about coffee with Starbucks founder Harold Schultz or motorcycles with Harley-Davidson turnaround leader Vaughn Beals?

The trio in Tampa who opened the first of over five hundred Outback Steakhouses had years of restaurant experience with Steak & Ale, Bennigan's, and Chili's and at the New Orleans World's Fair. This Australian concept restaurant has become one of the most popular and profitable steak houses of the decade.[7]

Home Depot founders Marcus and Blank acquired their expertise as senior executives at another home center called Handy Dan.

Any venture capitalist will tell you that the background and character of the people is the most important factor in the success of a new venture.

3

Attack by Stratagem

Strategic Rules
Win Without Fighting
Strength Against Weakness—Always
Beware of "High-Level Dumb"
Obey Fundamental Principles

At every level of any operation, strategy is indeed "war on a map"—it is the "plan on paper." Strategy deals with the allocation of resources to the battle. In *On War,* Clausewitz says that strategy sets the point *where,* the place *when,* and the *force with which* the battle is to be fought.

In his book *Strategy,* B. H. Liddell Hart explains the objective of strategy: "The true aim is not so much to seek battle as to seek a strategic situation so advantageous that if it does not of itself produce the decision, its continuation by battle is sure to achieve this."[1]

The first rule in strategy is to pay painstaking attention to the needs and wants of the customer and your organization's ability to fulfill those needs. This analysis includes every step from design through delivery and after-sale service. Only after a thorough analysis of your ability to meet the customer's needs do you check with competitive realities to determine the viability of your strategy. Great strategy never reacts to the competitor; instead, strategy defines the opportunity in terms of the customer and then considers the situation in the competitive environment. Strategy must also consider the depth of corporate resources, effect of government regulations, environmental concerns, and currency fluctuations.

Strategy is not a competitive game. "Do more, better, faster" is not a strategy. Strategy focuses on adding real value to the customer. Strategy does not seek confrontation; instead, it seeks to achieve objectives with minimum combat.

Great strategies arise from intense discussion and deliberation that take into account internal strengths and weaknesses and external threats and opportunities. This thorough analysis provides insights that can identify important strategic opportunities.

Win Without Fighting—Translation

Sun Tzu says:

Generally, in war the best thing of all is to take the enemy's state whole and intact; to ruin it is inferior to this. To capture the enemy's entire army is better than to destroy it; to take intact a battalion, a company or a five-man squad is better than to destroy them. Hence, to win one hundred victories in one hundred battles is not the acme of skill. To subdue the enemy without fighting is the supreme excellence.

Thus, the best policy in war is to attack the enemy's strategy. The second best way is to disrupt his alliances through diplomatic means. The next best method is to attack his army in the field.

The worst policy is to attack walled cities. Attacking cities is the last resort when there is no alternative.

It takes at least three months to make mantlets and shielded vehicles ready and prepare necessary arms and equipments. It takes at least another three months to pile up earthen mounds against the walls. The general unable to control his impatience will order his troops to swarm up the wall like ants with the result that one third of them are slain, while the cities remain untaken. Such is the calamity of attacking walled cities.

Therefore, *subdue the enemy's army without fighting. They capture the enemy's cities without assaulting them and overthrow his state without protracted operations.**

Their aim must be to take all under heaven intact through strategic superiority. Thus, their troops are not worn out and their triumph will be complete. This is the art of attacking by stratagem.

*Sun Tzu's Strategy Applied to Business

Subdue the enemy's army without fighting: Find a non-confrontational strategy.

Capture the enemy's cities without assaulting them: Use an indirect approach.

Overthrow his state without protracted operations: Win without expending excessive time or resources.

Win Without Fighting—Manager's Commentary

The ultimate victory is to win without conflict.

Holiday Inn established its initial success along well-traveled highways at the outskirts of towns, where it would not compete with major chain hotels like Hilton and Sheraton that were already established in city centers. Alamo Car Rental's first market entry was in the least crowded (and least alluring) niche of tour operators who purchased auto rentals at wholesale rates.

Across the television spectrum are companies who carved out a niche where there was limited competition: CNN in news, HGTV in home and garden ideas, MTV in music for the younger generation, the History Channel in documentaries, and the list goes on.

In the Philippines, Jolibee studied the marketing strategies of McDonald's in other countries and beat it to the marketplace. When the Big Mac arrived in Manila, it found competition firmly entrenched. Today, Jolibee outsells McDonald's in the Philippines.

Everyone with a new product or business concept has rushed to expand rapidly and capture markets ahead of competition. Witness the rapid expansion of Subway in sandwiches, Home Depot in home improvement, and Starbucks in coffee. The success of Beanie Babies is legendary.

The concept of being victorious without engaging in conflict is fundamental to Sun Tzu's strategic thought. To apply this concept, it is necessary to seek victory before entering the competitive arena. Otherwise, you must fight in the hope of winning. This concept of winning before the battle applies to every situation. We so often find that the outcome has really been determined before the battle. This is expressed in the saying: "The side that wins will be the side that has already won."

Strategy is *planning* process. It is war on paper. It is doing the right thing. It is seeking victory before the battle.

Tactics is a *contact* process. It is the action of the war. It is doing things right. It is the battle.

The best organizations develop win-win strategic initiatives. They do their planning (strategy) so well they are sure to win. When competitive forces are encountered, their implementation (tactics) is so good they win anyway.

Strength Against Weakness—Always—Translation

Sun Tzu continues:

Consequently, the art of using troops is this:

When 10 to the enemy's one, surround him.

When five times his strength, attack him.

If double his strength, engage him.

If equally matched, be capable of dividing him.

If less in number, be capable of defending yourself.

And if in all respects unfavorable, be capable of eluding him.

*Hence, a weak force will eventually fall captive to a strong one if it simply holds ground and conducts a desperate defense.**

*Other translators' versions of the last sentence help explain the consequences of fighting a larger foe:

A small force is but booty for one more powerful.

Samuel B. Griffith

Thus a small enemy that acts inflexibly will become captives of a large enemy.

Ralph D. Sawyer

For if inferior numbers make a determined stand, they will be captured by the greater.

A. L. Sadler

Though an obstinate fight might be made by a smaller force, in the end it must be captured by the larger force.

James Clavell

Note the phrases of warning to the smaller force: "if it simply holds ground," "acts inflexibly," makes "a determined stand," and "an obstinate fight." All suggest that guerrillas must be mobile and ready to "bug out" when outmatched.

Strength Against Weakness—Always—Manager's Commentary

Battles are won by concentrating strengths.

In America, Gillette will sell the most razor blades, Frito-Lay will sell the most potato chips, and Anheuser-Busch the most beer. The reason is simply they have more locations selling razor blades, potato chips, or beer. Their location strength is backed up with all the necessary strength of production and distribution.

Operations succeed because someone knows how to concentrate strengths against weaknesses. The rule of ratios of strengths is simple: if we do not have real superiority, we cannot win. The objective is not an equal match; seek an unequal advantage in your favor. As Napoleon said, "God is on the side of the heaviest artillery."

The issue is not one of raw numbers; superiority can be achieved in a variety of ways. In business competition, the superiority can be in elements of the marketing mix such as place (locations or shelf space), price, promotion, product, etc. Superiority can also be attained in the fighting spirit of the organization.

It is vital to know the strengths and weaknesses of our opponent in order to assess where the attack must be focused. Underestimate the opponent and the results can be disastrous.

The use of simple mathematical ratios to indicate when one should launch the offensive has a real application to every strategic situation.

When you have overwhelming superiority, you will win. When the other side has overwhelming superiority, it will win. Between these two extremes are a variety of situations where extended combat will be required.

Much of success in any endeavor can be achieved by focusing your resources where you can achieve decisive results profitably. You cannot be strong everywhere. This requires a careful analysis of both profit opportunities and market needs. The priority ranking is important. First, you must satisfy the needs of the market. Then, and only then, can you profit from your actions. When the profit requirements are first, you have the wrong decision sequence. The decision on the needs of the market is always made before the financial decision. It's done successfully no other way.

As you think about applying strength, think seriously about reinforcing your own strength. This is often the best way to win.

Beware of "High-Level Dumb"—Translation

Sun Tzu continues:
Now, the general is the bulwark of the state:
If the bulwark is complete at all points, the state will surely be strong.
If the bulwark is defective, the state will certainly be weak.
Now, there are three ways in which a sovereign can bring misfortune upon his army:

1. By ordering an advance while ignorant of the fact that the army cannot go forward, or by ordering a retreat while ignorant of the fact that the army cannot fall back. This is described as "hobbling the army."
2. By interfering with the army's administration without knowledge of the internal affairs of the army. This causes officers and soldiers to be perplexed.
3. By interfering with direction of fighting, while ignorant of the military principle of adaptation to circumstances. This sows doubts and misgivings in the minds of his officers and soldiers.

If the army is confused and suspicious, neighboring rulers will take advantage of this and cause trouble. This is simply bringing anarchy into the army and flinging victory away.

Orders Versus Instructions

In the Prussian armies of the late nineteenth century, a system was instituted to clearly differentiate between orders and instructions:

- *Instructions* were an expression of the commander's wishes, not to be carried out unless manifestly practicable.
- *Orders* were to be obeyed instantly and to the letter.

However, orders could be issued only by an officer *actually present with the troops concerned and fully aware of the situation.*[2]

This clear differentiation provides a methodology to ensure that headquarters does not run operations by remote control.

Beware of "High-Level Dumb"—Manager's Commentary

Avoid acting without full knowledge of the situation.

In *The Reckoning,* David Halberstam's book on the auto industry, he articulates the problem of "men whose strength was that they could hear the truth in their own voices." Halberstam says, "There were, it was believed, few honest answers at Ford during McNamara's years because there were few honest questions." I've observed that when managers do not ask the right questions, the answers do not make any difference. Obviously, this creates "high-level dumb" situations.

Do not sow the seeds of destruction by micromanaging. There are a variety of alibis for this behavior; none are valid! No subordinate can operate at a level of competency when the boss supervises every detail. Over one hundred years ago, Marshal Saxe wrote about generals who wish to do everything on the day of battle and as a result do nothing. Saxe says, "If the general wishes to be a sergeant-major and be everywhere, he will act like the fly in the fable who thought it was he that was driving the coach."

When management is incompetent, good people simply "fire their boss," as they leave the organization. High turnover rates can be a signal of trouble.

In *On the Psychology of Military Incompetence*, author Norman Dixon cites anxiety as the most common cause of leadership failure.[3] He theorizes that what has been taken for lack of intelligence was perhaps due to the crippling effects of anxiety on perception, memory, and thought.

Dixon identifies personal faults common to incompetence:

- A fundamental conservatism and clinging to outworn tradition
- A tendency to reject or ignore information
- A tendency to underestimate the opponent
- Indecisiveness
- A failure to make use of surprise
- A predilection for frontal assaults
- A failure to make adequate reconnaissance

Too often, incompetent leaders resist new information because it might cause them to change their course of direction. The greater the impact of the new information, the more strenuously it is resisted because if changes must be made, then they were wrong before.

Obey Fundamental Principles—Translation

Sun Tzu continues:

Thus, there are five points in which victory may be predicted:

1. He who knows when to fight and when not to fight will win.
2. He who understands how to handle both superior and inferior forces will win.
3. He whose ranks are united in purpose will win.
4. He who is well prepared and lies in wait for an enemy who is not well prepared will win.
5. He whose generals are able and not interfered with by the sovereign will win.

It is in these five points that the way to victory is known. Therefore, I say:

Know the enemy and know yourself, and you can fight a hundred battles with no danger of defeat.

When you are ignorant of the enemy but know yourself, your chances of winning and losing are equal.

If ignorant both of your enemy and of yourself, you are sure to be defeated in every battle.

Sun Tzu's Fundamental Principles Adapted for Business

1. Understand when to launch the offensive. Good information sources will help you know when to take offensive action and when to withhold it.
2. Allocate resources. Use different strategies when inferior and superior.
3. Plan a united effort. Secure a common belief at all levels in a common vision.
4. Take advantage of opportunities. Be prepared to act when others are unprepared.
5. Decentralize. Each unit leader must know his or her area and be empowered with authority.

Obey Fundamental Principles—Manager's Commentary

The chances for failure are high when the rules that ensure victory are ignored.

Here are a few fundamental principles of business:

Organize an Intelligence System: Know your market as well as you know yourself. Decision making must be data driven.

Maintain Objectives: Determine a clear direction and keep a steady aim. Do not wander down side tracks.

Establish a Secure Position: Strengthen your core competencies. Occupy a position that cannot easily be taken by your opponent.

Keep on the Offensive: Being on the offensive preserves freedom of action and keeps you in control.

Plan Surprise: This is the best way to gain psychological dominance and deny the initiative to your opponent. Speed is an essential component of surprise.

Think Maneuver: Consider how to put yourself at an advantage and your opponent at a disadvantage. Find lightly defended or unoccupied competitive positions.

Concentrate Resources: Mass sufficiently superior force at the decisive place and time. Be a guerrilla when you can't be a gorilla. The strongest at any given time and place will always defeat the weakest.

Practice Economy of Force: When you concentrate somewhere, you will be weak in other areas.

Keep It Simple: The simple works best. Even the simplest plans can be difficult to execute.[4]

These fundamental principles of business are guidelines that lead to success. Although principles can sometimes be violated, they must always be considered. To know the principles and violate them is to take risks. To ignore the principles is stupidity. Violate these principles only when you *know* you are violating them. The further you stray from the fundamental truths, the greater the risks.

Applying the principles is an art. It is in this art that judgment comes into play. Professionals are aware of the subtleties of business rules; amateurs too often ignore the rules. Both take risks; both win and lose. Only one has the odds in his favor. The greater the experience of the professional manager, the greater his or her understanding of the risks of straying from the principles and the less the tendency to stray without a valid reason.

4

Disposition of Military Strength

Strategic Rules
Be Invincible
Attain Strategic Superiority
Use Information to Focus Resources

In business discussions, the issue constantly arises: Does strategy determine tactics or is it tactics that determines strategy? Strategy *always* comes before tactics just as thinking comes before doing. However, thinking can be the easy part. It's the doing that is difficult.

It is a business fundamental that the strategy must be correct for the tactics to succeed. There's no chicken and egg problem here. The strategy must be right first; you must be *doing the right thing.* Then the tactics can support the strategy by *doing things right.* Excellent strategy at higher levels can sustain many tactical failures at lower levels. The converse is rarely true. Sustained tactical success—even continuous brilliant execution of tactics—seldom overcomes an inadequate strategic posture.

A bad strategy supported by good tactics can be a fast route to failure as, for example, driving fast and skillfully in the wrong direction will not get you to your destination. Success requires a balance of strategy and tactics. History proves that the best strategy and tactics are achieved in areas fundamental to the core strengths of the organization.

The strategic plan cannot be conceived in a tactical vacuum. Otherwise, the solution might parallel the plan of the mythical strategist who was asked for a strategy that would reduce the menace of German submarines. After some thought, the strategist declared, "Boil the ocean!" When asked how this could be accomplished, the impractical strategist replied, "That's for you to determine. I'm only a strategist."

Strategy must consider tactics, and successful tactical implementation requires an appreciation of strategy. Otherwise, the tactician will not understand why he or she is doing what. When we do not understand the underlying concepts, we do not have the ability to improve or improvise properly.

Be Invincible—Translation

Sun Tzu says:

The skillful warriors in ancient times first made themselves invincible and then awaited the enemy's moment of vulnerability. Invincibility depends on oneself, but the enemy's vulnerability on himself. It follows that those skilled in war can make themselves invincible but cannot cause an enemy to be certainly vulnerable. Therefore, it can be said that, one may know how to achieve victory, but cannot necessarily do so.

Invincibility lies in the defense; the possibility of victory in the attack. Defend yourself when the enemy's strength is abundant, and attack the enemy when it is inadequate.*

Those who are skilled in defense hide themselves as under the most secret recesses of earth.

Those skilled in attack flash forth as from above the topmost heights of heaven.

Thus, they are capable both of protecting themselves and of gaining a complete victory.

*Other translators offer different interpretations of invincibility:

So we see that the great general can protect himself from giving the enemy an opportunity for victory, but he cannot make the enemy susceptible to defeat.

Brian Bruya

Invincibility is a matter of defense, vulnerability is a matter of attack. Defense is for times of insufficiency, attack is for times of surplus.

Thomas Cleary

Security against defeat implies defensive tactics; ability to defeat the enemy means taking the offensive. Standing on the defensive indicates insufficient strength: attacking a superabundance of strength.

Lionel Giles

Defend yourself when you cannot defeat the enemy, and attack the enemy when you can. One defends when his strength is inadequate; he attacks when it is abundant.

General Tao Hanzhang

Be Invincible—Manager's Commentary

Build strengths that can take advantage of opportunities.

The invincible awards in American business go to companies like Microsoft, with its take no prisoners attitude; McDonald's, which is everywhere; and Starbucks, which owns the high ground in gourmet coffee. The list goes on.

A common characteristic of these premier organizations is a strong founding leader who set the direction and kept the organization on course. Strong companies are founded by strong individuals—when they leave, the stamp of their culture becomes the core of the organization's future.

At Ogilvy & Mather, founder David Mather established the practice of sending each new branch head a nested set of wooden dolls—each doll opens to reveal a smaller replica of the doll. Inside the smallest is a message, "If each of us hires people who are smaller than we are, we shall become a company of dwarfs; but if each of us hires people who are bigger than we are, Ogilvy & Mather will become a company of giants."[1]

Personal leadership is where "art" takes over to control the application of "science." This does not mean that principles are ignored but rather that the successful leader understands how to properly apply the principles.

The ultimate success of the organization is dependent on the inspiration and leadership of the executive at the highest level. Using the authority the position commands, the senior leader can set in motion a chain of events that will cascade changes throughout the entire organization. Effecting these changes and making them work require a leadership style dramatically different from the old paradigm.

No leader does it alone. As Kets de Vries points out in *Life and Death in the Executive Fast Lane:* "The derailment of a CEO is seldom caused by a lack of information about the latest techniques in marketing, finance, or production; rather, it comes about because of a lack of interpersonal skills—a failure to get the best out of people who possess necessary information."

Coca-Cola has a chief learning officer whose job is to figure out how to institutionalize the sharing of experiences between branch offices, countries, and people, and to turn Coke into a "learning organization." "The ability to learn faster than your competitors may soon be the only sustainable competitive advantage," says Arnie De Geus, head of planning at Royal Dutch Shell.[2]

Attain Strategic Superiority—Translation

Sun Tzu continues:

To foresee a victory no better than ordinary people's foresight is not the acme of excellence. Neither is it the acme of excellence if you win a victory through fierce fighting and the whole empire says, "Well done!" Hence, by analogy, to lift an autumn hair [hare] does not signify great strength; to see the sun and moon does not signify good sight; to hear the thunderclap does not signify acute hearing.

In ancient times, those called skilled in war conquered an enemy easily conquered. Consequently, a master of war wins victories without showing his brilliant military success, and without gaining the reputation for wisdom or the merit for valor. He wins his victories without making mistakes. Making no mistakes is what establishes the certainty of victory, for it means that he conquers an enemy already defeated.

Accordingly, a wise commander always ensures that his forces are put in an invincible position, and at the same time will be sure to miss no opportunity to defeat the enemy. *It follows that a triumphant army will not fight with the enemy until the victory is assured, while an army destined to defeat will always fight with the opponent first, in the hope that it may win by sheer good luck.** The commander adept in war enhances the moral influence and adheres to the laws and regulations. Thus it is in his power to control success.

*Other translators emphasize the importance of strategic planning:

Thus, a victorious army wins its victories before seeking battle; an army destined to defeat fights in the hope of winning.

Samuel B. Griffith

So we see, the victorious person creates the conditions for certain victory and then does battle with the enemy. The defeated person always engages the enemy first, then hopes he is lucky enough to win.

Brian Bruya

Attain Strategic Superiority—Manager's Commentary

A successful strategy achieves victory before the battle.

There is a long history of the successful entry of products where competition was minimal or nonexistent: Xerox into copiers, IBM into data analysis, Apple into home computers, and Crest with fluoride toothpaste. With this kind of superiority, the initial competitive battle was quite limited in scope.

Milwaukee-based Kohl's has cut a wide swath in soft goods retailing with a leadership dedicated to a carefully crafted strategy. A stock analyst says, "Kohl's combines the cost structure of a discounter and the brands of a department store. It straddles those worlds and takes share from both." The design and merchandising is not too upscale and not too low rent. The shopper finds a clean bright store where everything is easy to find. The service is good and the perceived value is high.[3]

The introduction of Tide detergent by Procter & Gamble involved a classic strategy of gaining brand name superiority. When automatic washers first came to market, manufacturers were anxious to educate new purchasers to use detergent instead of soap, which would leave a scum in places that could not be cleaned. So P&G provided leading producers with free boxes of Tide to be packed in every automatic washer at the factory. The free trial experience convinced many to become repeat customers. And Tide became the leading detergent brand without engaging in a major conflict.

Although all conflict cannot be avoided, a well-planned strategy will nullify most opposition. Fighting and winning requires less strategic skill than winning without fighting.

Opportunities for attaining strategic superiority can be found in:

- The product or service that is so clearly unique and carefully targeted that it is has no competition.
- The idea that is so completely researched and validated that no other seems viable.
- The fundamental truth that is presented with such moral strength that any other approach appears immoral.

The issue is always how one's strategy can win the customer and nullify the opposition. The offensive should never be aimed at the opponent's strengths. Strategies that focus on the customer's needs and consider the opponent's weaknesses have the best odds for winning.

Use Information to Focus Resources—Translation

Sun Tzu continues:

*Now, the elements of the art of war are first, the measurement of space; second, the estimation of quantities; third, the calculation of figures; fourth, comparisons of strength; and fifth, chances of victory.**

Measurements of space are derived from the ground. Quantities derive from measurement, figures from quantities, comparisons from figures, and victory from comparisons.

Therefore, a victorious army is as one yi balanced against a grain, and a defeated army is as a grain balanced against one yi.

An army superior in strength takes action like the bursting of pent-up waters into a chasm of a thousand fathoms deep. This is what the disposition of military strength means in the actions of war.

*Other translators clarify:

The art of war may be summarized into five steps:
First, survey of terrain features;
Second, decision of the plan of campaign;
Third, calculation of man-power;
Fourth, weighing of chances;
Fifth, deliberation on victory.

Tai Mien-leng

According to *The Art of War,* there are five processes of preparation:

1. to control,
2. to produce,
3. to compare,
4. to determine,
5. to win.

Tang Zi-chang

Use Information to Focus Resources—Manager's Commentary

Use data to plan overwhelming advantages.

Robert Nardelli, president of General Electric's power systems unit, asked his top one hundred customers about their most critical needs and how GE could provide solutions. The answers prompted the company to drastically reduce its response time for providing parts. It also opened the opportunity to advise utilities on the nuances of expanding into foreign markets that were new to them but not to GE.[4]

At Ford's monthly strategy meetings, data is reviewed on the profitability and growth potential of Ford's broad line of car and truck models. This information on the customer's preferences is used to rapidly and surgically eliminate products that are no longer in demand.

When the *Arizona Republic* learned that readers didn't have time or patience to wade through long features, it added boxes summarizing the content. When subscribers to the Long Island *Newsday* complained they weren't getting their papers early enough, the operation was reengineered to provide 5:30 A.M. delivery.[5]

In each of these examples, data links the customer's preferences to performance improvements. Customer input is a vital component of an organization-wide performance measurement system.

Organizations that have added only customer input to their historic financial measurements have not completed their system. Although the customer input adds another dimension, the financial measures only serve to keep score on what has happened. More is needed.

The solution is to focus on defining and aligning performance in several key areas: financial, customer, employee, process, innovation, and learning. With achievement of the corporate strategy as the main objective, supportive objectives are established for each key performance area at every level of the organization. Then, a measurement system to track performance is cascaded so that everyone is aligned to achieve the desired results. This cascading measurement system, often called a balanced or synchronized scorecard, encourages the kind of performance that achieves results in areas critical to success.

This balanced system of measurements is a dynamic, continuous activity where all processes are aligned with strategy. To put it simply, linking your vision to performance improves productivity and profit potential.

5

Use of Energy

Strategic Rules
Build a Sound Organization Structure
Apply Extraordinary Force
Coordinate Momentum and Timing

There are two basic command systems for the use and control of energy in the attack:

> *Centralized Control—Reinforcing Weakness:* Imagine a field of battle where the commander monitors the front line to see where he is winning and losing. When he sees that one of his units is losing, he sends in reserves to strengthen the weakness. This system of reinforcing weakness requires a high degree of control.
>
> *Decentralized Control—Reinforcing Strength:* In this situation, as offensive forces move forward, they attempt to bypass strengths instead of engaging in battle. If the offensive forces meet opposition, they go around again and again until they find where they can penetrate. The front line commander does not ask for permission to advance; he merely reports while the senior commander and his staff monitor and support the advance. This decentralized control reinforces strength.[1]

The decision to use a system of centralized or decentralized control depends on the mental set of the senior officers and the corporate culture. Whether the culture tolerates one system or the other has a great deal to do with success.

Someone must be in charge. Where everyone decides everything, no one decides anything. Rule by committee can become rule by mediocrity.

Chaos is the inevitable result when decisions are made by everyone. Clearly expressing his views on command, Napoleon wrote to the National Assembly stating that one bad general is preferable to two good ones.

Be careful! The ability of modern communications to reach everywhere can make it too easy to concentrate all power in a single person, who through overwork is often over his or her head.

No one command system is best. Command systems radically different from each other have led to equally good results.

Build a Sound Organization Structure—Translation

Sun Tzu says:

Generally, management of a large force is the same in principle as the management of a few men: it is a matter of organization. And to direct a large army to fight is the same as to direct a small one: it is a matter of command signs and signals.*

*In general, commanding a large number is like commanding a few. It is a question of dividing up the numbers. Fighting with a large number is like fighting with a few. It is a question of designation and configuration.

Ralph D. Sawyer

Organizational Warnings

In 210 B.C. Petronius Arbiter wrote: "We trained hard, but it seemed that every time we were beginning to form up in teams we would be reorganized. I was to learn later in life that we tend to meet any new situation by reorganizing, and a wonderful method it can be for creating the illusion of progress while producing confusion, inefficiency, and demoralization."

Over a hundred years ago, a French officer, Ardant du Picq, warned:

Note the army organizations and tactical formations on paper are always determined from a mechanical point of view, neglecting the essential coefficient, that of morale. They are almost always wrong. . . . Mental acquaintanceship is not enough to make a good organization. A good general esprit is needed.

In his book, *Generalship: Its Diseases and Their Cure*, J. F. C. Fuller wrote: "The horde army paralyzed generalship, not so much because it changed tactics, but because it prevented tactics changing."

Discussing the resulting staff structure, he said: "The general alone is responsible, therefore the general alone should and must decide and must elaborate his own decisions and not merely have them thrust on him by his staff like a disc upon a gramophone."

Build a Sound Organization Structure—Manager's Commentary

The organization exists so that tasks can be managed, people supported, and results achieved.

At Harley-Davidson, the organization chart is three overlapping circles: a Create Demand Circle responsible for marketing and sales, a Produce Products Circle for engineering and production, and a Support Circle for all other functions. In the middle where the circles intersect is a Leadership and Strategy Council that oversees general management functions like planning, budgeting, and human relations. The overlapping of the circles emphasizes the interdependence between areas and encourages participation and collaboration.[2]

At Xerox, a three-level organization chart shows the corporate staff at the bottom supporting the business teams and districts at the top. Profit and loss responsibility rests with the business team general managers.

At one of the world's largest service companies, Rentokil, in England, the lean headquarters staff is untypical of a company that employs 150,000 people. The organization is managed through branch offices operating as independent profit centers.

No single organization structure works everywhere.

In his book, *Creating Change-Capable Cultures*, Gerald Sentell says, "Structure is to an organization as channels are to river systems. They direct and control flows of human interaction and activity. . . . When the structure can contain and direct the flows of behavior, the system functions. When the flows jump out of the structured channel, the results can create great change."[3]

When organizations are structured to maximize strengths within departments, the result can disrupt the overall optimization of the organization. When departments are organized to serve themselves, the sum total of these departmental kingdoms is not maximized to serve the customer—and business is lost to competitors who know how to focus strengths on the customer.

Systems and processes should not be designed to accommodate the strengths and weaknesses of individuals. Instead, the requirements of the system determine where people are placed in the structure.

Structure follows strategy, always. First determine the strategy to achieve your vision, and then develop the organization structure. Finally, put the best people in place.

Apply Extraordinary Force—Translation

Sun Tzu continues:

That the whole army can sustain the enemy's all-out attack without suffering defeat is due to operations of extraordinary and normal forces. Troops thrown against the enemy as a grindstone against eggs is an example of the strong beating the weak.

Generally, in battle, use the normal force to engage and use the extraordinary to win.[*] Now, to a commander adept at the use of extraordinary forces, his resources are as infinite as heaven and earth, as inexhaustible as the flow of the running rivers. They end and begin again like the motions of the sun and moon. They die away and then are reborn like the changing of the four seasons.

There are not more than five musical notes, but the various combinations of the five notes bring about more melodies than can ever be heard.

There are not more than five basic pigments, yet in blending them together it is possible to produce more colors than can ever be seen.

There are not more than five cardinal tastes, but the mixture of the five yields more flavors than can ever be tasted.

In battle, there are not more than two kinds of postures—operation of the extraordinary force and operation of the normal force, but their combinations give rise to an endless series of maneuvers. For these two forces are mutually reproductive. It is like moving in circle, never coming to an end. Who can exhaust the possibilities of their combinations?

*Translators offer a variety of meanings for what this version calls the normal and the extraordinary:

- One translates the Chinese ideograms as meaning *direct and indirect*—that is, use the direct to engage, the indirect to win.
- Another calls the normal force *regular operations* and the extraordinary force *surprise.*
- Still another says, *In fighting you engage the foe with the main body and defeat him with the reserves.*

Apply Extraordinary Force—Manager's Commentary

Use the normal to engage, the extraordinary to win.

Frito-Lay knows how to apply extraordinary force at the point of sale with drivers who restock customers' shelves with uncommon frequency. With the extraordinary force of over two million agents knocking on doors, Avon is the world's number one direct seller of cosmetics. BMW's extraordinary effort takes a different approach in Retail 2000, which teams a single BMW representative with the customer during ownership. Cyberspace is turning storefront retailing into the normal force and Internet retailing into the extraordinary.[4]

Virgin and its founder, Richard Branson, are masters of the extraordinary. From the publicity generated by luxurious airport lounges and comfortable airplane seating to headline grabbing stunts like hot-air ballooning, Branson knows how to use the extraordinary to build a brand image and extend it to music, cola, vodka, and financial services.

This powerful idea of moving from the normal to the extraordinary achieves results at every level and in every situation. The classic human relations case study occurred years ago at the Bell Lab Hawthorne plant when researchers determined that giving extraordinary attention to a small group of workers increased production. This study concluded that production went up regardless of whether working conditions were enhanced or made worse. The key was the extraordinary attention. Today, results are being achieved by people-oriented activities that apply the extraordinary. It may be as simple as applying teamwork to problem solving, finding new ways to get commitment, or initiating training programs.

The idea of using *the extraordinary* is an extremely simple concept that clearly identifies what must be done to win. Too often, our plans are based on using only the normal force, and the result is that only "normal" results are achieved. Every annual plan that simply adds "some effort" to what was done last year is only another dance. It takes the force of extraordinary effort to achieve extraordinary results.

The idea of using extraordinary force does not mean more of the same effort. Extraordinary action results from out-of-the-box thinking. Major General J. F. C. Fuller writes, "If we wish to think clearly, we must cease imitating. If we wish to cease imitating, we must make use of our imagination. Audacity and not caution must be our watch word."

Coordinate Momentum and Timing—Translation

Sun Tzu says:

When torrential water tosses boulders, it is because of its momentum; when the strike of a hawk breaks the body of its prey, it is because of timing.* Thus, in battle, a good commander creates a posture releasing an irresistible and overwhelming momentum, and his attack is precisely timed in a quick tempo. The energy is similar to a fully drawn crossbow; the timing, the release of the trigger. Amid turmoil and tumult of battle, there may be seeming disorder and yet no real disorder in one's own troops. In the midst of confusion and chaos, your troops appear to be milling about in circles, yet it is proof against defeat.

Apparent disorder is born of order; apparent cowardice, of courage; apparent weakness, of strength. Order or disorder depends on organization and direction; courage or cowardice on postures; strength or weakness on dispositions.

Thus, one who is adept at keeping the enemy on the move maintains deceitful appearances, according to which the enemy will act. He lures with something that the enemy is certain to take. By so doing he keeps the enemy on the move and then waits for the right moment to make a sudden ambush with picked troops.

Therefore, a skilled commander sets great store by using the situation to the best advantage, and does not make excessive demands on his subordinates. Hence he is able to select the right men and exploits the situation. He who takes advantage of the situation uses his men in fighting as rolling logs or rocks. It is the nature of logs and rocks to stay stationary on the flat ground, and to roll forward on a slope. If four-cornered, they stop; if round-shaped, they roll. Thus, the energy of troops skillfully commanded is just like the momentum of round rocks quickly tumbling down from a mountain thousands of feet in height. This is what "use of energy" means.

*Other translators clarify the meaning of the first sentence:

That the velocity of cascading water can send boulders bobbing about is due to its strategic advantage. That a bird of prey when it strikes can smash its victim to pieces is due to timing.

Roger Ames

The onset of troops is like the rush of a torrent which will even roll stones along its course. The quality of decision is like the well-timed swoop of a falcon which enables it to strike and destroy its victim.

Lionel Giles

Coordinate Momentum and Timing—Manager's Commentary

Momentum provides force; timing applies strength at the right moment.

Subway opened 10,000 stores in the last decade and today sells sandwiches from over 13,000 franchised stores in 64 countries—a momentum that makes Subway second only to McDonald's in number of outlets.[5]

General Electric has been on a roll for years and is keeping its momentum in sales and profits going with as many as seventy-five acquisitions in a single year.

Nothing succeeds like success, and success generates its own momentum. The mini-van and the sports utility vehicle were successful products for the early innovators. This timely innovation of desirable product concepts created its own momentum.

Just as volume sales create momentum and enthusiasm, so does obsolete inventory stifle innovation and growth. When the cash register rings, it seems like you are doing everything right. When it doesn't ring, the mistakes are very visible.

Successful strategic thrusts are achieved by rapidly accumulating power (momentum) and releasing that power when it will have the most desirable effect (timing). A typical business application would be the introduction of a very competitive new product or the implementation of a major change in warranty or pricing at a major trade show, when it would be most disruptive of a competitor's plans.

Momentum and timing are most often combined in advertising campaigns where massive expenditures are timed with seasonal demand. Or as an associate often said when we discussed timing of a major event, "Let's go hunting when the birds are flying."

The simultaneous use of multiple principles or techniques, a concept the military refers to as force multipliers, can apply a lot of pressure. It is not that victory is achieved with the application of a single principle, but rather the use of multiple principles achieves a reinforcing momentum. The cumulative effort of doing a lot of right things right multiplies into awesome power! This happens when retailers move into a new market with multiple locations featuring extensive selections, and engage in enough advertising to make them a super power in the media.

6

Weakness and Strength

Strategic Rules
Take the Initiative
Plan Surprise
Gain Relative Superiority
Seek Knowledge
Be Flexible

Achieving real superiority is fundamental to the concept of strength against weakness. Your strategy and tactics must be designed with the idea that your competitor will not have anywhere near an equal chance to win. Strategically, the concentration of strength against weakness is a mental process. Tactically, this concentration is a physical act.

Here are key methodologies for concentrating strength against weakness:

Flank: Concentrate strength against weakness by launching an end run around strong points to a lightly defended or unoccupied position. In your search for weakness, consider these two key elements:
- Look for weakness at a junction. It can be between geographic locations or product lines. Also explore going around the extreme low end or high end of a product category.
- Since every strength has a corresponding weakness, look for the weakness of the opposition's strength.

Segment: This is concentrating strength in a specific area. The small can never equal the big everywhere, but anyone can be strong somewhere. As markets have been segmented and resegmented, marketers discover new ways to concentrate against weakness and then concentrate again into a smaller niche or particle market.

Overwhelm: Any initiative can be achieved if enough strength is concentrated to support it. Conversely, any initiative can be defeated if enough strength is focused against the weakness of that initiative.

Reinforce: The best odds for success are achieved by spending time, money, and energy reinforcing what is working. Then you are leveraging off what you do well.

Take the Initiative—Translation

Sun Tzu says:

Generally, he who occupies the field of battle first and awaits his enemy is at ease; he who arrives later and joins battle in haste is weary. And, therefore, one skilled in war brings the enemy to the field of battle and is not brought there by him.*

One able to make the enemy come of his own accord does so by offering him some advantage. And one able to stop him from coming does so by inflicting damage on him.

Therefore, on the day the decision is made to launch war, you should close the passes, destroy the official tallies, and stop the passage of all emissaries. Examine the plan closely in the temple council and make final arrangements.

If the enemy leaves a door open, you must rush in. Seize the place the enemy values without making an appointment for battle with him. Be flexible and decide your line of action according to the situation on the enemy side.

At first, then, exhibit the coyness of a maiden until the enemy gives you an opening; afterwards be swift as a running hare, and it will be too late for the enemy to oppose you.

*The one who first decides on the battleground and there awaits the enemy has the easier task, and the one who comes after and has to hurry will tire himself. The good fighter makes others move, but is not made to move by them.

A. L. Sadler

Seize and Maintain the Initiative

Mao Tse-tung wrote: "No military leader is endowed by heaven with an ability to seize the initiative. It is the intelligent leader who does so after a careful study and estimate of the situation and arrangement of the military and political factors involved."

In *The Foundations of Strategy*, Captain Johnstone warned: "The initiative, once handed over to the enemy, is hard to regain: Ward off blows for a week and your hands are full of defensive details, you begin to be apprehensive of the unseen work of the enemy, and you abandon your plan on small provocation."

Take the Initiative—Manager's Commentary

By its very nature, the offensive offers an advantage for gaining superiority.

"Intel Inside" was one of the first brand name campaigns in the technology industry, and today Intel ranks high on *Financial World*'s list of brand valuations. The perception is that an Intel processor inside your PC means having reliable, state-of-the-art technology.

Minnesota Mining & Manufacturing (3M) generates about one-third of its sales revenues from new products that did not exist four years ago. In a single year, 3M received over five hundred U.S. patents for new products. It accelerates sales with a Pacing Plus initiative that rapidly develops and markets the most promising new products aimed at high growth industries.[1]

In a relatively short time, Starbucks has successfully transformed one of the world's most commonplace beverages into a premium product sold in over a thousand stores. Starbucks continues to expand its initiative by forming alliances with airlines, hotels, distributors, and retailers.[2]

The most effective and decisive way to reach the objective is to seize, retain, and exploit the initiative. Being on the offensive puts you in control and forces the opponent to react.

Taking the initiative is first a strategic mental process followed by real tactical action. By acting first, we preserve freedom of action. If our opponent moves first, our only choice may be to react.

The attack has the advantage of initiative. It often forces action on our opponent and relegates him to second place. Initiating the offensive adds positive morale to our side.

The keys to the successful initiative are skill, preparation, and information. The norm is not enough time, not enough resources, not enough information. Consequently, the initiative often requires that "great mental leap in the dark."

Only rarely will exact details be known. While the attempt to get more information is made as a matter of course, waiting for news in a difficult situation is a bad error. While data is needed to launch the offensive, normally the sooner that something is done, the better will be the odds in your favor, and the better will be the results.

Beware! The offensive does not offer a solution to all problems. Your desire for action must be matched by wisdom.

Plan Surprise—Translation

Sun Tzu continues:

Thus, when the enemy is at ease, he is able to tire him; when well fed, to starve him; when at rest, to make him move. All these can be done because you appear at points which the enemy must hasten to defend.

That you may march a thousand li without tiring yourself is because you travel where there is no enemy.

That you are certain to take what you attack is because you attack a place the enemy does not or cannot protect.

That you are certain of success in holding what you defend is because you defend a place the enemy must hasten to attack.

Therefore, against those skillful in attack, the enemy does not know where to defend, and against the experts in defense, the enemy does not know where to attack. *

How subtle and insubstantial that the expert leaves no trace. How divinely mysterious that he is inaudible. Thus, he is master of his enemy's fate.

His offensive will be irresistible if he plunges into the enemy's weak points; he cannot be overtaken when he withdraws if he moves swiftly. Hence, if we wish to fight, the enemy will be compelled to an engagement even though he is safe behind high ramparts and deep ditches. This is because we attack a position he must relieve.

If we do not wish to fight, we can prevent him from engaging us even though the lines of our encampment be merely traced out on the ground. This is because we divert him from going where he wishes.

*Another translator expands on how to confuse opponents:

Thus, an ingenious attacker makes the defender at a loss how to defend; an ingenious defender makes the attacker at a loss how to attack.

Zhang Huimin

Plan Surprise—Manager's Commentary

*Blend subtlety and secrecy to keep the opponent confused
so he knows neither where to attack or defend.*

Southwest Airlines often waits until the last moment to announce plans to extend its routes to new markets so that competition has little time to prepare.

The importers of upscale champagne, Dom Perignon, use secrecy as a part of their strategy. One of their executives who refused to talk about how they market their product said, "We don't want to talk about Dom Perignon. We want to maintain its mystique."

Getting information about what's happening in Iraq may be easier than finding out what's happening at Mars candy headquarters.

Secrecy about your own movements can be more threatening to competitors than overt action. Some manufacturers have a corporate policy of no public announcement preceding a new product introduction. Since the unknown often appears more threatening than the known, this secrecy becomes a powerful and threatening ally. Concerning corporate raider Rupert Murdoch, a Wall Street analyst said, "Part of Murdoch's strategy is to play his cards close to his vest. The magic is secrecy."

Secrecy protects your plans, while surprise confuses your opponent. In business, it is not essential that your opponent be taken unaware, but only that he becomes aware too late to react effectively. In that case, your opponent will probably announce that he "misread the market."

Even though your current position may be weak, you can do things to divert the enemy from your position. This kind of bluff is achieved by starting rumors that work to your advantage.

The objective of surprise is to obtain a psychological dominance that denies the initiative to your opponent. Sheridan said the reason for Grant's victories in the Civil War was that "while his opponents were kept fully employed wondering what he was going to do, Grant was thinking most of what he was going to do himself." When surprise is achieved, the balance of power will often be decisively shifted. As a result, success earned from surprise greatly exceeds the effort expended.

Speed is an essential component of surprise. The longer you take, the more likely your opponent will be aware of your actions. Focus on rapid, hard-hitting thrusts aimed at your opponent's weakness.

Gain Relative Superiority—Translation

Sun Tzu continues:

Accordingly, by exposing the enemy's dispositions and remaining invisible ourselves, we can keep our forces concentrated, while the enemy's must be divided. We can form a single united body at one place, while the enemy must scatter his forces at 10 places. Thus, it is 10 to one when we attack him at one place, which means we are numerically superior. And if we are able to use many to strike few at the selected place, those we deal with will be in dire straits.

The spot where we intend to fight must not be made known. In this way, the enemy must take precautions at many places against the attack. The more places he must guard, the fewer his troops we shall have to face at any given point.

For if he prepares to the front his rear will be weak; and if to the rear, his front will be fragile. If he strengthens his left, his right will be vulnerable; and if his right gets strengthened, there will be few troops on his left. If he sends reinforcements everywhere, he will be weak everywhere.

Numerical weakness comes from having to prepare against possible attacks; numerical strength from compelling the enemy to make these preparations against us.

Relative Superiority Wins

The concept of relative superiority can be distilled from Sun Tzu's statement: ". . . *we can keep our forces concentrated, while the enemy's must be divided.*" Another translation is worded: ". . . *if I concentrate while he divides, I can use my entire strength to attack a fraction of his.*"

In the first millennium during the Song dynasty, China had the biggest and strongest army in the world. However, the leaders did not trust their army and ignored Sun Tzu's advice on concentration by splitting their forces between capital and border armies. As a result, they lost to the Mongol invaders who could concentrate their strength against fractions of the Chinese.

In *On War*, Clausewitz says, "Where absolute superiority is not attainable, you must produce a relative one at the decisive point by making skillful use of what you have."

Gain Relative Superiority—Manager's Commentary

Deploy resources to concentrate strengths against weaknesses.

Known as the "Killer Bs," Barnes & Noble and Borders have swept across America opening six hundred superstores in five years and driving hundreds of small bookstores out of business.

Bookstores that continue to thrive have found a niche where they can achieve relative superiority. In a megastore built long before the chains came to Portland, Oregon, Powell's main bookstore stocks 200,000 titles of new books (a third more than the average Barnes & Noble) plus 300,000 used books. New and used books are stacked side by side so that readers find an awesome selection in every category. Says Michael Powell, "One way to survive is simply to be bigger and offer a more diverse stock than they do." In addition to the giant main store, Powell's has six satellite stores and kiosks in a nursery, hospital, and hardware store—all acting as feeders to the main store.[3]

An inferior force can think strategically about winning if it can tactically achieve relative superiority at each point of contact. This is the way small companies become big companies and competitors in every endeavor become champions. This is the way guerrillas win—they find out where the enemy is weak and overwhelm him at that point.

When you attempt to concentrate everywhere, you have no concentration. The more thoroughly you specialize, the more sure you are to win. Winning strategies mass resources on the main effort and allocate minimal resources to secondary efforts.

Relative superiority is the best strategy for most companies. Although relative superiority is most often thought of as weight of numbers, there is a variety of ways to achieve relative superiority:

- Implementing continuous action—for example, consistent, small ads
- Segmenting by finding a niche or particle market
- Concentrating on your own strengths
- Forming an alliance—for example, joining a franchise
- Achieving superior product or service quality

When you cannot have absolute superiority, you must concentrate your strengths against your opponent's weaknesses to achieve relative superiority. It's a business fundamental that you must focus your resources where you can achieve decisive results profitably.

Seek Knowledge—Translation

Sun Tzu continues:

Therefore, if one knows the place and time of the coming battle, his troops can march a thousand li and fight on the field. But if one knows neither the spot nor the time, then one cannot manage to have the left wing help the right wing or the right wing help the left; the forces in the front will be unable to support the rear, and the rear will be unable to reinforce the front. How much more so if the furthest portions of the troop deployments extend tens of li in breadth, and even the nearest troops are separated by several li!

Although I estimate the troops of Yue as many, of what benefit is this superiority in terms of victory?

Thus, I say that victory can be achieved. For even if the enemy is numerically stronger, we can prevent him from fighting.

Therefore, analyze the enemy's battle plan, so as to have a clear understanding of its *strong and weak points. Agitate the enemy so as to ascertain his pattern of movement. Lure him in the open so as to find out his vulnerable spots in disposition. Probe him and learn where his strength is abundant and where deficient.**

Now, the ultimate in disposing one's troops is to conceal them without ascertainable shape. In this way, the most penetrating spies cannot pry nor can the wise lay plans against you.

*Here is another translator's version of getting more knowledge about your opponent's plans:

Scheme so as to discover his plans and the likelihood of success. Rouse him, and learn the principle of his activity and inactivity. Force him to reveal himself, so as to find out his vulnerable spots. Carefully compare the opposing army with our own, so that you may know where strength is superabundant and where it is deficient.

Tang Zi-chang

Seek Knowledge—Manager's Commentary

Knowledge helps stack the odds in your favor.

When Ford introduced the Taurus, engineers tore apart competitors' cars to find features to adapt. In an extensive research campaign, Ford went to end customers and dealers' sales and service personnel to find out what customers wanted. Eventually, a want list of over fourteen hundred items was generated. About 50 percent of these "wants" were incorporated in the Taurus, which became one of the hottest selling new cars of its time.

When Gillette decided to become the premier male grooming authority, it sought to really understand the male customer and his needs. Gillette's research showed that customers wanted better quality, technology, and performance. This knowledge led to developing more advanced shaving systems that reinforced its premier image goal.

Knowledge of the current situation makes it possible for victory to be created. As Patton said, "Intelligence is like eggs, the fresher, the better."

Here are active ways to produce the kinds of knowledge about your opponent that help determine the correct strategy for winning:

- *Watch what he is doing.* As Yogi Berra said, "You can see a lot by observing."
- *Watch what he is not doing.* This is key to obtaining relative superiority.
- *Probe.* This reveals the opponent's strengths and weaknesses.
- *Benchmark.* This gets people involved in finding out how to develop the best processes.

Centuries ago, Ovid wrote, "It is right to learn, even from the enemy."

Basic to success in business is being close to the customer. That's why executives visit the marketplace. They realize they must not only understand how the customer thinks, they must be able to think like a customer. It is essential to know what your customer wants. The idea of gathering and analyzing information before the battle hasn't been tried and found wanting; it's been found difficult and not tried.

In *The Exceptional Executive*, Levinson says, "A professional is a person who must understand and apply scientific knowledge. Unless he does so, he will be buffeted by forces beyond his control. Given knowledge, the professional can choose courses of action. He is in charge of himself and his work." Absolutely nothing beats using data to make decisions.

Be Flexible—Translation

Sun Tzu continues:

*Even though we show people the victory gained by using flexible tactics in conformity to the changing situations, they do not comprehend this.** People all know the tactics by which we achieved victory, but they do not know how the tactics were applied in the situation to defeat the enemy. Hence no one victory is gained in the same manner as another. The tactics change in an infinite variety of ways to suit changes in the circumstances.

Now, the laws of military operations are like water. The tendency of water is to flow from heights to lowlands. The law of successful operations is to avoid the enemy's strength and strike his weakness. Water changes its course in accordance with the contours of the land. The soldier works out his victory in accordance with the situation of the enemy.

Hence, there are neither fixed postures nor constant tactics in warfare. He who can modify his tactics in accordance with the enemy situation and thereby succeeds in winning may be said to be divine. Of the five elements, none is ever predominant; of the four seasons, none lasts forever; of the days, some are longer and others shorter, and of the moon, it sometimes waxes and sometimes wanes.

*Other translators give their interpretations of the need for flexibility:

Perfectness of military movement lies in variation; it is beyond the prying of subtle spies and the machinations of wise brains.

Tai Mien-leng

Victory is won by flexibly coping with circumstances. If you lay this fact before the people, they will find it hard to comprehend.

Zhang Huimin

Be Flexible—Manager's Commentary

While strategies remain constant, tactics must be adapted to each new situation.

Mervyn's department store chain uses a SWAT team of organizational commandos to manage unpredictable staffing needs, meet the needs of erratic market swings, and seize unanticipated opportunities. The SWAT team members must have expertise in buying, merchandising, or advertising. They go where needed on assignments ranging from one week to six months. Exhibiting a bias for action, they ask questions, assess situations, and solve problems.[4]

When P&G spent too long in test markets, competitors watched its time-consuming testing process and moved rapidly to beat it to the market rollout with copycat products.

The opposite side of the coin of flexibility is rigidity. When we are rigid, we are predictable. In competitive battles, predictability can be a weakness. Being predictable can signal your intended actions to your opponent, and the odds of failure increase.

Winning isn't easy; it requires simultaneous planning and action. While preliminary planning is important, too much planning can be deadly. All plans are merely the basis for change. Revise plans in relation to what is happening and make adjustments as you go.

The blitzkrieg (lightning war) used so successfully by the German army in World War II is an adaptation of Sun Tzu's comments about the flow of water around obstacles. The blitz is launched along a wide front with the objective of rapid penetration. When resistance is met, the forces go around until they can get through.

The blitz in any business operation works the same way. It is a concentrated effort in a short period of time with the objective of going around resistance and focusing resources where results can be attained. The blitz requires a high degree of decentralization. Forget remote approvals; the successful blitz is an empowered front line offensive with results that can far exceed any ordinary effort. You can find the "lightning war" concept applied throughout organizations in everything from a productivity-oriented kaizen blitz to a volume-oriented sales blitz.[5]

7

Maneuvering

Strategic Rules
Maneuver to Gain the Advantage
Achieve the Critical Mass
Deceive Your Competitor
Develop Effective Internal Communications
Gain the Mental Advantage

At the strategic level, maneuvering is a way of thinking about how you are going to act in a manner that puts your opponent at a disadvantage. At the tactical level, maneuvering most frequently involves concentrating or dispersing as you seek the most advantageous route. Without thinking about how to maneuver, the idea of fighting when outnumbered is ludicrous.

The way to avoid what is strong is to attack what is weak. Look for lightly defended positions. Engage in a frontal attack only when you have overwhelming superiority. However, sheer numbers and firepower alone are often not enough to dislodge a competitor in an entrenched position.

Look for situations where real superiority can be attained. In business, as in any battle, the best approach is most often the one that achieves superiority at the decisive point. The marketing maneuver is often an indirect approach to where your customers are and your competitors aren't.

One of the best maneuvers can be to relocate the battle. When an advertising executive arrived at a presentation, he found his client thinking of hiring a new agency. He switched from his prepared presentation to a discussion of what the client needed to do to succeed. Afterwards, he commented, "I didn't even talk about the competitive account; I merely changed the battleground."

In all disagreements, including corporate political situations, thinking about maneuvering turns the mind to options. It takes the focus away from confrontation and refocuses on selecting a route that increases the odds of winning. The best win is a maneuver to a win-win.

Product line extensions of dry prepared pet foods were Ralston-Purina's maneuver to dominance on the grocery shelf. Dog chow was followed by puppy chow; then came cat chow and kitten chow flavors—all side-by-side.

Maneuver to Gain the Advantage—Translation

Sun Tzu says:

Normally, in war, the general receives his commands from the sovereign. During the process from assembling the troops and mobilizing the people to deploying the army ready for battle, nothing is more difficult than the art of maneuvering for seizing favorable positions beforehand. *What is difficult about it is to make the devious route the most direct and to turn disadvantage to advantage.** Thus, forcing the enemy to deviate and slow down his march by luring him with a bait, you may set out after he does and arrive at the battlefield before him. One able to do this shows the knowledge of artifice of deviation.

Thus, both advantage and danger are inherent in maneuvering for an advantageous position.

*The difficulty in battles is in turning the circuitous into the straight and turning reverses into advantages.

A. L. Sadler

Here are military maneuvers adapted for business:

Frontal Attack: Head-on attack with overwhelming superiority.
Attack in Echelon: Initiate the attack with the strongest products or
    services; then follow up with weaker ones.
Flanking Attack: Attack lightly defended or unoccupied positions.
Blitz: A concentrated effort that keeps on moving as strong points are
    bypassed.

Encirclement: Launch a variety of competitive products and/or deny key resources to your opponent.

Fabian: Refuse to compete in certain areas, attack in others.

Defense: Maintain position against competitive thrusts.

Relocate the Battle: Find a new competitive arena.

Guerrilla: Find a niche and take what you can get when you can get it.

Retreat: Get out of business.

General Pogo's Strategy: He said, "We have met the enemy and they is us." Attack yourself first.[1]

Maneuver to Gain the Advantage—Manager's Commentary

The longest way around can be the shortest route to success.

Major victories have been won by doing the impossible through the impassable. By figuring out how to do the impossible of getting a package from one office to another overnight, Federal Express founder Fred Smith maneuvered to a unique position in the market. And when competition began encroaching on FedEx's "overnight" turf, it redefined overnight to mean "before 10:30 A.M." At the same time, FedEx set up a tracking program so it could rapidly answer questions concerning the en route location of every package. By innovating this new system of early delivery and tracking, FedEx established difficult obstacles for competitors who wanted to achieve parity in service. FedEx has continued its maneuvers to provide services that give it an advantage. Now you can get your FedEx package delivered in many markets before 8 A.M. or on Sunday. As one wag said, "I use FedEx when I 'absolutely, positively' want my package to get there on time and the U.S. Post Office when I 'kind of, sort of' want timely delivery."

Maneuvering to find an advantage is important in every competitive situation. In the auto wars, the Germans did not attack the American cars head-on; they maneuvered to the lightly defended flank at the low end of the market with the Volkswagen and at the high end with BMW and Mercedes. The Japanese copied this tactic, first with brands at the low end and then continually maneuvered upwards until they reached the high end.

Since the easiest routes are often the most heavily defended, the longest way around can indeed be the shortest way home. The courses of action which appear most advantageous usually contain the seeds of disadvantage. For example, if you take too long to get organized, you will probably arrive too late. However, if you are not organized, your efforts will be too fragmented to win.

The key to success is turning a circuitous route into a straight route for you alone. Move rapidly; the longer you are en route, the more difficult it may be to get your resources to the market before your competitor.

Extended warranties have been a successful maneuver to a position of product or service superiority for many organizations. Although this works only until your competitor establishes parity, it can be a preemptive maneuver to win customers.

Achieve the Critical Mass—Translation

Sun Tzu continues:

One who sets the entire army in motion with impedimenta to pursue an advantageous position will be too slow to attain it. If he abandons the camp and all the impedimenta to contend for advantage, the baggage and stores will be lost.

It follows that when the army rolls up the armor and sets out speedily, stopping neither day nor night and marching at double speed for 100 li to wrest an advantage, the commander of three divisions will be captured. The vigorous troops will arrive first and the feeble will straggle along behind, so that if this method is used only one-tenth of the army will arrive. In a forced march of 50 li the commander of the first and van division will fall, and using this method but half of the army will arrive. In a forced march of 30 li, but two-thirds will arrive. Hence, the army will be lost without baggage train; and it cannot survive without provisions, nor can it last long without sources of supplies.

One who is not acquainted with the designs of his neighbors should not enter into alliances with them. Those who do not know the conditions of mountains and forests, hazardous defiles, marshes and swamps, cannot conduct the march of an army. Those who do not use local guides are unable to obtain the advantages of the ground.

Strategic initiatives can be either sequential or cumulative:

A *sequential initiative* requires planned, consecutive steps to achieve success. A new product launch requiring orderly introduction to the sales force, trade channels, and end customers would most often be a sequential strategy. So would a plan to initiate a new program over time in successive units.

A *cumulative initiative* is the result of a series of random actions piling on top of one another until at some undetermined point the critical mass is reached. The brand manager who uses sponsorship and events to build brand awareness is often using a cumulative strategy as is the plant manager who initiates a quality campaign in units throughout the plant.[2]

Achieve the Critical Mass—Manager's Commentary

Apply overwhelming force at the decisive place and time.

By concentrating in four product areas and acquiring over eighty companies, Dennis Kozlowski, chief executive of Tyco International, raised market capitalization from $2 billion to $30 billion in six years. Organizations like Ingersoll-Rand and United Dominion Industries who have been diversified are successfully focusing their strengths on three or four key business sectors.

Many companies who thought they were in the computer hardware business have been beaten by companies who understood the importance of being in the software business. Witness the rise of Microsoft.

For years, one of the major buying decisions of gasoline station owners was which brand of gasoline pump to buy. Then as the convenience store component of the gas station emerged, these storeowners found they needed merchandise sales recorded through a software system. The gas pump (hardware) buying decision became secondary to the more important software buying decision that provided a full range of inventory and sales information.

Strategic initiatives must focus on the critical factors that give you a competitive advantage. When you have a unique enough advantage, you should be able to get 100 percent of the market.

The critical mass is simply the concentration of energy required to achieve success. What counts is not only the strength of resources, but the speed with which it is delivered. That energy concentration can be in any facet of the organization; for example, purchasing, production, marketing, distribution, etc. Sara Lee, whose products are number one or two in every category, is concentrating on marketing. It is a cake company without ovens, a merchandiser of Hanes hosiery without knitting mills, and a seller of Ball Park franks without processing plants.

In every situation, understanding the critical mass helps you find a solution. The story is told about the person who was trying to convince his friend to gamble. He said, "Give me five reasons why you don't want to gamble." The friend replied, "The first is I don't have any money." Back came the response, "Forget the other four!" Indeed the critical mass was money.

In business as in nuclear fission, a concentration of energy must be attained to achieve the critical mass. The manager must focus his or her energy on performance of the tasks most critical to success.

Deceive Your Competitor—Translation

Sun Tzu continues:

Now, war is based on deception. Move when it is advantageous and change tactics by dispersal and concentration of your troops.* When campaigning, be swift as the wind; in leisurely march, be majestic as the forest; in raiding and plundering, be fierce as fire; in standing, be firm as the mountains. When hiding, be as unfathomable as things behind the clouds; when moving, fall like a thunderclap. When you plunder the countryside, divide your forces. When you conquer territory, defend strategic points.

Weigh the situation before you move. He who knows the artifice of deviation will be victorious. Such is the art of maneuvering.

*Other translators clarify the meaning of deception:

In warfare, practice dissimulation, and you will succeed. Move only if there is a real advantage to be gained. Whether to concentrate or divide your troops, must be decided by circumstances.

Lionel Giles

When waging war, you must employ cunning tactics and multiple transformations in order to succeed. You must judge whether or not something is advantageous before you act. You must decide whether to concentrate your troops or divide them according to circumstances.

Brian Bruya

Forces achieve missions with unexpectation, take advantage to fit advantages, and create diversity through scattering and regrouping.

J. H. Huang

Deceive Your Competitor—Manager's Commentary

Deception is always targeted at the competitor—never the customer.

In baseball, deception is part of the surprise throw to catch the runner off base; in football, it's the hidden ball play; in basketball, it's the faked pass. Why should we consider deception unsportsmanlike in business competition?

Contemporary managers may wonder about Sun Tzu's emphasis on the importance of deception. Any deceptive action might seem to be immoral. In business, the subtle difference is that deception is practiced to confuse the competitor—never the customer.

A South American company and a competitor agreed to maintain high prices on a new product both were introducing. After a few months the competitor cut prices in violation of the agreement causing a loss of business. When questioned, the competitor replied that it reduced prices to increase sales. The victimized company was not aware of the admonition from an ancient strategist who said, "Do not do what your enemy wants, if for no other reason than he wants it."

Much of the success of the invasion of Europe in World War II was the result of deception. This misinformation succeeded so well that when the actual invasion took place, the German officers thought the invaded beaches were the deception.

You have often seen deception used as a tactic in negotiations. One side attempts to gain a psychological advantage by appearing to be naive and uninformed when, in fact, it is smart and knowledgeable.

Another deceptive approach in negotiation is to appear to be dejected and crestfallen about your opportunity for prevailing. An opponent who thinks he or she is winning is likely to be overconfident and vulnerable. Developer John Thornton knew he had the right to match the best offer in a bankruptcy sale. To keep his competitor's offer low, Thornton acted dejected, put his house up for sale, and wore the same suit for three days. His opponent was stunned when Thornton appeared in court and matched the best offer.

Secrecy can also be a means of achieving deception. This forces your opponent to second-guess your next move. The bigger you are, the more psychologically threatening the unknown becomes to your opponent.

The only thing better than having your opponent not know what you are doing is to have him or her think you are planning to do something entirely different from what you really intend to do. This is deception. Go for it.

Develop Effective Internal Communications—Translation

Sun Tzu continues:
The book of Army Management says: "As the voice cannot be heard in battle, gongs and drums are used. As troops cannot see each other clearly in battle, flags and banners are used." Hence, in night fighting, usually use drums and gongs; in day fighting, banners and flags. Now, these instruments are used to unify the action of the troops. When the troops can be thus united, the brave cannot advance alone, nor can the cowardly retreat. This is the art of directing large masses of troops.

Simple Communications Work Best

In Sun Tzu's time, the only available communications were quite simple. Today, we have a wide range of communications methods available and use them all. Invariably, people at the bottom complain about lack of communication, and people at the top complain about receiving more information than they can process.

With computers, the solution to more communications capacity is to break the problem into segments and look at each segment. With people, the solution is a similar decentralization. You break down the problem and achieve decisions by the people at each level instead of sending it all to the top where you overload the head person's brain. With decentralization, you lessen the need for communications at every level.

Regardless of the level, simplicity clears the mind. Keep in mind the rule of three: never make more than three points about an issue. The problem is that long lists are confusing and, as a result, nothing is remembered. As an example, here are three facts concerning a nineteenth century Prussian command system:

1. An army cannot be effectively controlled by direct orders from headquarters.
2. The man on the spot is the best judge of the situation.
3. Intelligent cooperation is of infinitely more value than mechanical obedience.[3]

Develop Effective Internal Communications—Manager's Commentary

Implement ways to get messages received and understood.

Sears tracked the links in the chain of cause and effect running from employee attitude to customer behavior to profit. It modeled how an improvement in employee attitude changed behavior. The better behavior created an improved customer impression that resulted in a measurable increase in revenue.

Awareness of this employee-customer-profit linkage made Sears management determined to give every employee the information needed to develop an enlightened opinion about how to do his or her job better. Town meetings were held to spread the word and get employees initiating improvements. A corporate university was established. All of the training was focused on changing employee perceptions and attitudes so that attention and behavior would be focused on customers. As operating managers changed their behavior toward employees, front line employees changed their behavior toward customers.[4]

Note the sequence: The change in behavior at the management level caused the change in behavior at the front line. Behavior is a form of communication. Management must walk the talk.

At Wal-Mart headquarters, a managers meeting every Saturday morning provides the opportunity for office and field managers to share successful ideas. The following Monday, field managers fly out, and the new ideas explode throughout the chain.

In every industry we receive and process so much information so fast that it's easy to hear only what we want to hear. It's becoming increasingly difficult to break through the clutter and get our message communicated to our own people.

Effective internal communication happens only as the result of a well-designed plan. This plan is organized around the understanding that all messages are not delivered in the same manner. Good news may need to be delivered only once to be heard. Instructions and changes that disrupt existing paradigms must be communicated in several different ways and often repeated before people will accept the new information. In these instances, a single method of communication is not enough; every message needs to be reinforced by using different methodologies such as one-to-one meetings, department meetings, and interactive forums.

Gain the Mental Advantage—Translation

Sun Tzu continues:

A whole army may be robbed of its spirit, and its commander deprived of his presence of mind. Now, at the beginning of a campaign, the spirit of soldiers is keen; after a certain period of time, it declines; and in the later stage, it may be dwindled to nought. *A clever commander, therefore, avoids the enemy when his spirit is keen and attacks him when it is lost.* * This is the art of attaching importance to moods. In good order, he awaits a disorderly enemy;

in serenity, a clamorous one. This is the art of retaining self-possession. Close to the field of battle, he awaits an enemy coming from afar; at rest, he awaits an exhausted enemy; with well-fed troops, he awaits hungry ones. This is the art of husbanding one's strength.

He refrains from intercepting an enemy whose banners are in perfect order, and desists from attacking an army whose formations are in an impressive array. This is the art of assessing circumstances.

Now, the art of employing troops is that when the enemy occupies high ground, do not confront him uphill, and when his back is resting on hills, do not make a frontal attack. When he pretends to flee, do not pursue. Do not attack soldiers whose temper is keen. Do not swallow a bait offered by the enemy. Do not thwart an enemy who is returning homewards. When you surround an army, leave an outlet free. Do not press a desperate enemy too hard. Such is the method of using troops.

*Other translators give their interpretations of the use of morale:

A large army may be robbed of its morale and a general may be robbed of his resolution . . . a good strategist makes a point of shunning the keen morale of the enemy and does not strike him until his morale has run out.

Zhang Huimin

So you should take away the energy of their armies, and take away the heart of their generals . . . avoid the keen energy and strike the slumping and receding.

Thomas Cleary

Gain the Mental Advantage—Manager's Commentary

Understand the psychological factors affecting human resources.

Opportunities for victory are found in the mental capacity of the leader to integrate strategy (planning) and tactics (execution). The ultimate responsibility for victory or defeat lies with the leader, not because the leader must do everything, but because he or she must have the mental capacity and provide the means to translate sound strategy into successful tactics.

Externally, the mental advantage is achieved through surprise. You must generate a mismatch by getting inside your adversary's observation-orientation-decision-action time cycle. By the time your adversary observes what he or she thinks you are doing, becomes oriented to it, decides what to do, and takes action, "it" will be too late.

Internally, several key issues are basic to good management psychology:

Attitude: A positive outlook and a cool head are the foundation of a good attitude.

Morale: Napoleon said, "The moral is to the physical as three is to one." The word "moral" refers to a worthwhile cause, a belief that what we are fighting for is just and right. It is the "moral cause" that produces high morale.

   The moral issues required in business are both the moral courage to make the right decisions and act on them, and the leadership style that helps make everyone feel good about himself or herself. The business equivalent of military courage is confidence. However, confidence must be based on knowledge and experience.

Physical: Keep yourself physically fit and nurture a healthy business environment.

Adapt to Circumstances: No plan can see beyond the first engagement. Although it is important to follow the plan, it is equally important to know when and how to modify the plan.

Rewards: Internal motivators include profit sharing, gain sharing, glory sharing, and fame sharing. The simple pat on the back can accomplish much.

Yogi Berra purportedly said about baseball, "Ninety percent of this game is half mental." How often we hear that golf and tennis are mental games. So it is in business. The mental advantage begins with the warm confidence of a positive attitude.

8

Variation of Tactics

Strategic Rules
Consider Tactical Options
Prepare Adequate Defenses
Avoid the Faults of Leadership

S trategy determines direction. The actual execution of the plan to achieve objectives is called tactics and it begins with contact. Internally, that contact may be with the development or production process of a product or service. Externally, that contact is usually with a customer. The contact makes personal relationships an important issue in tactics and explains why tactics must vary. At the point of contact, unpredictable personal equations become part of the scenario.

While strategic principles are unchanging for all time, tactics (implementation of the strategy) vary with the times and circumstances and must be tuned to current situations.

The purpose of tactical maneuvering is to relocate the battle to a place where superiority can be obtained. In a study of 300 military campaigns, in only six was a decisive result achieved by a direct frontal approach to the main army of the enemy. Why would the results of a frontal attack be any different in other kinds of campaigns? Although the idea is appealing, the highly touted "head-on attack" has been consistently unsuccessful. The most successful tactics are usually based on some form of maneuver.

Strategies at any level are the tactics of the next lower level in the chain of command. The best tactical school is experience. And the people with prior experience in their industry have the soundest tactical foundation.

As you shape tactical options, focus on the customer. The key to success is *what the customer wants*, not what you can do. What ConAgra could do tactically in frozen foods was low-cost mass production. What the customer wanted was healthy foods with great taste. To develop the Healthy Choice brand to meet the customer's taste standards, ConAgra sent food technologists to the Culinary Institute. The result: a successful new brand that dominates the market.

Consider Tactical Options—Translation

Sun Tzu says:

Generally, in war, the general receives his commands from the sovereign, assembles troops, and mobilizes the people. When on grounds hard of access, do not encamp. On grounds intersected with highways, join hands with your allies. Do not linger on critical ground. In encircled ground, resort to stratagem. In desperate ground, fight a last-ditch battle.

There are some roads which must not be followed, some troops which must not be attacked, some cities which must not be assaulted, some ground which must not be contested, and some commands of the sovereign which must not be obeyed.

Hence, the general who thoroughly understands the advantages that accompany variation of tactics knows how to employ troops.

The general who does not is unable to use the terrain to his advantage even though he is well acquainted with it. In employing the troops for attack, the general who does not understand the variation of tactics will be unable to use them effectively, even if he is familiar with the Five Advantages.

A wise general in his deliberations must consider both favorable and unfavorable factors. *By taking into account the favorable factors, he makes his plan feasible; by taking into account the unfavorable, he may avoid possible disasters.**

*Other translators explain favorable factors as opportunity or advantage:

In the midst of difficulties we should ever be ready to grasp every opportunity so that our object may be obtained. In a favorable situation, we should be alert in detecting our weakness so that we may avoid misfortune.

Tai Mien-leng

If our expectation of advantage be tempered, we may succeed in accomplishing the essential part of our schemes. If, on the other hand, in the midst of difficulties we are always ready to seize an advantage, we may extricate ourselves from misfortune.

Lionel Giles

Consider Tactical Options—Manager's Commentary

Victory depends on our strength, which we control, and the opportunities provided by our opponent, which we cannot control.

At Microsoft, senior managers meet nightly in a triage meeting during the final months of the software development process. Triage is a ruthless assessment that determines priorities for immediate action. In the Microsoft meeting, managers representing all perspectives are engaged in a power interchange. People voice their point of view, and the group negotiates a decision. Trade-offs are made clear by the key question: "Is this the hill we want to die on?" Decisions are immediately communicated so everyone can get on with his or her work.[1]

Philip Knight, cofounder of Nike, wrote a graduate thesis at Stanford University. The title was: "Can Japanese Sport Shoes Do to German Sport Shoes What Japanese Cameras Did to German Cameras?" A year later he was in the shoe business—the rest is history. He knew where he wanted to go and had a sense of how he could adopt different tactics in the sports shoe business.

Because victory is dependent upon both our actions and those of our opponent, maximum effort does not ensure a competitive victory. This situation can be readily seen in every sporting event where maximum effort on the playing field is exerted by every participant. There are winners and losers in every game.

Tactical flexibility is the hallmark of many organizations with a reputation for customer service. That is, within guidelines, associates are empowered to take whatever action is necessary to serve the customer.

In the complexity of the business environment, an organization may be on the offensive with one product or service and on the defensive with another. The same strategies and tactics cannot be used for all circumstances. The question is how much time the manager should spend shoring up weaknesses as opposed to maximizing strengths. The options differ depending upon whether we are attacking or defending. The low-cost competitor and the high-end producer often have different core strengths requiring different tactics. The differences become obvious when you scan the advertising messages in a newspaper or magazine.

Regardless of the circumstances, the spirit of the offense must always prevail. At Fort Donelson, when General Grant found his army half-routed, he galloped down the line shouting, "Fill your cartridge boxes quick and get into line; the enemy is escaping and must not be permitted to do so."

Prepare Adequate Defenses—Translation

Sun Tzu continues:

What can subdue the hostile neighboring rulers is to hit what hurts them most; what can keep them constantly occupied is to make trouble for them; and what can make them rush about is to offer them ostensible allurements.

It is a doctrine of war that we must not rely on the likelihood of the enemy not coming, but on our own readiness to meet him; not on the chance of his not attacking, but on the fact that we have made our position invincible.*

*Other translators comment on preparing a defense:

Fundamentals in the use of forces are: do not rely on their not approaching, but rely on our readiness against them; do not rely on their not attacking, but rely on our readiness which cannot be attacked.

J. H. Huang

Do not depend on the enemy not coming; depend rather on being ready for him. Do not depend on the enemy not attacking; depend rather on having a position that cannot be attacked.

Roger Ames

Strengthening the Defense

Strengthening the defense does not mean maintaining the status quo. After the machine gun had been in use for some time, the French Chief of Infantry said to Parliament, "Make no mistake, this weapon will change nothing." General John J. (Black Jack) Pershing noted that the arrival of the airplane provided an excellent and efficient means of getting oats to horses![2]

Too often what happens in the implementation of new military and business tools (i.e., quality management) is that the new is simply overlaid on old doctrine and structure. World competition is a powerful new force moving quickly to challenge keepers of the old paradigm. But human nature being what it is, there will always be a struggle to maintain the status quo.

Prepare Adequate Defenses—Manager's Commentary

The best defense is a good offense.

"We will encircle Caterpillar and become the dominant producer in the industry," declared Komatsu a decade ago. Many observers predicted that Caterpillar would join the long list of American corporations that have fallen to the Japanese.

After surviving Komatsu's attack, Donald Fites, chairman and CEO of Caterpillar, said, "The biggest reason for Caterpillar's success has been our system of distribution and product support and the close customer relationships it fosters." The backbone of that system is a long history of quality relationships by Caterpillar with its world network of independent dealers. So when Komatsu's attack began, the strongest unit of defense, the dealer structure, was in place. Of course, this alone was not enough to overcome Komatsu's cost advantage; Caterpillar also had to make the organization flatter, meaner, and leaner. However, Komatsu could not overcome the marketing strength provided by Caterpillar's network of dealers with strong customer contacts. Understanding the strength of personal relationships has long been a weakness of the Japanese. The strong defense of high-quality dealer relationships and support has brought Caterpillar to the point where its share of the world market for construction and mining equipment is the highest in its history.[3]

Smaller companies or brands have achieved a good defense by owning very strong positions in a niche or particle segment of a product line or business. When they own a position in the customer's mind, they can hold off the big competitors. Witness Maker's Mark in bourbon, Danner in boots, and regional grocers or pizza parlors in your home town.

Even on the defensive, the rule is to seek every opportunity to seize the initiative and achieve results by offensive action. When you are constantly in a defensive posture, you can seldom win. If you stop the attack, there will be another one.

Too often, the strategy that strengthens the defense is characterized by finding some way to redesign your existing product instead of getting out in front of the trend or technology. The mistake is to try to serve the old market in a new way instead of going where the market is growing. The defensive is not achieved by building better buggy whips.

Avoid the Faults of Leadership—Translation

Sun Tzu continues:
   There are five dangerous faults that may affect a general:

   If reckless, he can be killed;
   if cowardly, captured;
   if quick-tempered, he can be provoked to rage and make a fool of himself;
   if he has too delicate a sense of honor, he is liable to fall into a trap because of an insult;
   if he is of a compassionate nature, he may get bothered and upset.*

   These are the five serious faults of a general, ruinous to the conduct of war. The ruin of the army and the death of the general are inevitable results of these five dangerous faults. They must be deeply pondered.

*Other translators' versions of the faults that may affect a general:

1. Recklessness, which leads to destruction;
2. Cowardice, which leads to capture;
3. A hasty temper, which can be provoked by insults;
4. A delicacy of honor, which is sensitive to shame;
5. Over-solicitude for his men, which exposes him to worry and trouble.

Lionel Giles

1. Those who are ready to die can be killed;
2. Those who are intent on living can be captured;
3. Those who are quick to anger can be shamed;
4. Those who are puritanical can be disgraced;
5. Those who love people can be troubled.

Thomas Cleary

Avoid the Faults of Leadership—Manager's Commentary

Flaws in the personal character of the commander will cause opportunities to be lost.

"Chainsaw" Al Dunlap got his reputation by staging massive cutbacks in personnel at Scott Paper. When the same approach didn't work at Sunbeam, he tried sales and accounting gimmicks to bolster results. Soon he was asked to exit.

Jim McCann, as president of 1-800-FLOWERS, tells about the lesson he learned from General Electric CEO Jack Welch. McCann had to fire a senior person that everyone knew wasn't right for the job. The guy was a friend, and the prospect of action was brutal. He met Welch at a dinner party and told him about the situation. Welch's response was, "When was the last time anyone said, 'I wish I had waited six months longer to fire that guy?'"[4]

Peers and subordinates will discover the ineffective manager long before his or her seniors do. The dysfunctional interactions resulting from the discovery will reduce this person's effectiveness—and the effectiveness of the organization.

Here are business parallels to Sun Tzu's character flaws:

Reckless (meaning no forethought): The reckless manager does not understand how to use data. He or she shoots from the hip. When a win is achieved, it is simply because he or she did something, rather than because the right thing was done.

Cowardly (self-protective or afraid): The person who is afraid to take risks, takes the greatest risk of all. This manager is like McClellan in the Civil War who was so fearful of losing he could not win.

Quick-Tempered (too easily angered): Reference has been made to the importance of a cool head. Managers who have a reputation for shooting the messenger don't often get bad information and don't know what is really going on.

Delicate Honor (exaggerated sensitivity): The business parallel here is being too easily embarrassed, taking things personally, or letting ego get in the way.

Too Compassionate (too concerned): Those who have this fault are so concerned about the reactions of people that short-term decisions are made to keep harmony. The result is these managers end up with a long-term disaster. In their compassion people are often left "twisting slowly in the wind" when the kindest thing that could be done is to make the hard decision.

9

On the March

Strategic Rules
Occupy Strong Natural Positions
Always Seek the High Ground
Make an Estimate of the Situation
Discipline Can Build Allegiance

Strategically, a secure position establishes a base for the offensive. Tactically, this secure position helps you use your natural strengths. Positions where you can occupy a key strong point are important in every endeavor. There are only a few leaders in each industry; everyone else marches in their shadow.

In order for a position to be secure, we must "own" it. We "own" a position because of a perceived strength—the perception *is* indeed the reality. People accept only that which is consistent with what they already know as they add to their perceptions about the position of a product or service.

All positions are in the mind, and the entry into the mind is through emotions, not logic. Logic sounds most convincing to the presenter; it is in the emotions of the receiver that positions are changed. In thinking about attacking competitive positions, the first rule is: it's very, very difficult to move into a position occupied by someone else.

To build a strong position, you must first determine what position you want and who you want your customers to be. Then figure out how you are going to meet the needs of those potential customers better than anyone else.

In business, the most secure positions are owned by those who achieve a base of loyal customers. Premier positions are earned by organizations that have systems for really listening to their customers. They then focus resources on meeting or exceeding needs in a manner that delights customers. The idea is to make customers so happy that not only do they not buy anything else, they don't even *think* of buying anything else.

However, the more secure your position seems to be, the greater can be the danger. When you feel most secure, you are most vulnerable to surprise.

Occupy Strong Natural Positions—Translation

Sun Tzu says:

Generally, when an army takes up a position and sizes up the enemy situation, it should pay attention to the following:

When crossing the mountains, be sure to stay in the neighborhood of valleys; when encamping, select high ground facing the sunny side; when high ground is occupied by the enemy, do not ascend to attack. So much for taking up a position in mountains.

After crossing a river, you should get far away from it. When an advancing invader crosses a river, do not meet him in midstream. It is advantageous to allow half his force to get across and then strike. If you wish to fight a battle, you should not go to meet the invader near a river which he has to cross. When encamping in the riverine area, take a position on high ground facing the sun. Do not take a position at the lower reaches of the enemy. This relates to positions near a river.

In crossing salt marshes, your sole concern should be to get over them quickly, without any delay. If you encounter the enemy in a salt marsh, you should take position close to grass and water with trees to your rear. This has to do with taking up a position in salt marshes.

On level ground, take up an accessible position and deploy your main flanks on high grounds with front lower than the back. This is how to take up a position on level ground. These are principles for encamping in the four situations named. By employing them, the Yellow Emperor conquered his four neighboring sovereigns.

In *The Science of War,* Colonel Henderson wrote:

". . . by no means sufficient importance is attached to the selection of positions . . . and to the immense advantages that are to be derived from the proper utilization of natural features."

Occupy Strong Natural Positions—Manager's Commentary

Find the strength of natural positions that cannot easily be occupied by your opponents.

Experienced travelers know that Singapore Airlines is one of the best overseas carriers and Midwest Express has the most comfortable domestic coach seats. Travelers also know that Ritz-Carlton and Four Seasons have earned natural high-end positions in lodging and Fairfield and Hampton Inns are in sound value-priced positions.

In Beijing, China, a member of the government travel service commented to me about hotels, saying, "Our hardware is better than our software." He was referring to the new hotel buildings as the better hardware and the service experience as the poorer performing software. When the overall perception is of mediocre service, no physical elegance will change that position.

Marks & Spencer dominates retailing in England the way no one company does in the United States. Every week 14 million people walk into one of its 250 stores. Its Marble Arch store is in the *Guinness Book of Records* for the most volume per square foot. Everything in the store is sold under one brand name, St. Michael. With this single, private brand, Marks & Spencer sells 40 percent of the underwear and 20 percent of all hosiery sold in England.

Many companies are gaining strength by going back to their roots. At these core positions they have the most inherent natural strength.

The perception of what we "are" is based on what we "have been." Over time, the perception of what we "are" matches what we "really are." We, ourselves, or our product or service can't be something else. Everyone who has tried to win by copying has failed. The failure in copying is often caused by not understanding the subtleties. To change your position in the customer's mind over time, you must change who you really are.

Efforts focused on reinforcing your natural position make it easier to communicate your position. When you say that you are what you really are, the believable message gets through to your audience.

Going up the positioning ladder to achieve a stronger share of mind requires a well-conceived and executed plan. Coming down is what happens when you are not going up. Ask any former sports star like good old "what's his name."

Always Seek the High Ground—Translation

Sun Tzu continues:

Generally, in battle and maneuvering, *all armies prefer high ground to low,** and sunny places to shady. If an army encamps close to water and grass with adequate supplies, it will be free from countless diseases and this will spell victory. When you come to hills, dikes, or embankments, occupy the sunny side, with your main flank at the back. All these methods are advantageous to the army and can exploit the possibilities the ground offers.

When heavy rain falls in the upper reaches of a river and foaming water descends, do not ford and wait until it subsides. When encountering "Precipitous Torrents," "Heavenly Wells," "Heavenly Prison," "Heavenly Net," "Heavenly Trap," and "Heavenly Cracks," you must march speedily away from them. Do not approach them. While we keep a distance from them we should draw the enemy toward them. We face them and cause the enemy to put his back to them.

If in the neighborhood of your camp there are dangerous defiles or ponds and low-lying ground overgrown with aquatic grass and reeds, or forested mountains with dense tangled undergrowth, they must be thoroughly searched, for these are possible places where ambushes are laid and spies are hidden.

*Ordinarily, the force prefers heights and hates the lowlands.

R. L. Wing

The High Ground

The most desirable position in war has always been the high ground controlling the surrounding terrain. Frederick the Great referred to selection of positions as the talent of great men—the ability immediately to conceive all the advantages of the terrain. He said, "The first rule that I give is always to occupy the heights."

Always Seek the High Ground—Manager's Commentary

The high ground is the strongest position.

The high ground in business today is owned by names with brand strength like Microsoft in software, Coca-Cola in soft drinks, Nike in athletic shoes, and McDonald's in fast foods.

Attaining the high ground is one battle and keeping it is another. In the battle for dominance of browsers in the World Wide Web, Netscape got to the high ground in market share by giving away free product. Then Microsoft entered the market with free software while Netscape started to charge for its browser and down went Netscape's market share.

Apple gained the high ground in desktop publishing and image/graphic handling ability. Then it frittered this leadership position away through complacent, arrogant tactics. Now it's fighting back for a stronger position.

Jelly Belly, with 75 percent of the gourmet jelly bean market, is trying to increase its market share even more by selling through major grocery chains. The concern is that this expanded distribution may affect the brand name cachet and upset its current distribution channels.

Each of these brands faces the problem that market share is either increasing or decreasing. There's no such thing as staying exactly where you are. You either get bigger or you get smaller.

In the military, positioning is occupying a key strong point in the terrain. In business, positioning is occupying a key strong point in the mind. You "own" a position in the mind either because you are the leader or because of significant differentiation. The unique taste of Dr. Pepper provides a significant differentiation, as does the unique marketing approach of Ben & Jerry's ice cream.

The worst position of all may be not having a position. That's the problem experienced by people in the struggling brand name you've never heard about. In the final analysis it is the perceptions of the market that actually position the brand.

In every industry, the action of moving up in market share erodes the competitor's base. This dysfunction forces displaced competitors to compete for lesser positions that offer even smaller profits. As market positions change, the one who captures higher ground gets the larger revenue base and all the accompanying advantages. Similarly, the loser's losses are cumulative—negatively.

Make an Estimate of the Situation—Translation

Sun Tzu continues:

When the enemy is close at hand and remains quiet, he is relying on a favorable position. When he challenges battle from afar, he wishes to lure you to advance; when he is on easy ground, he must be in an advantageous position. When the trees are seen to move, it means the enemy is advancing; when many screens have been placed in the undergrowth, it is for the purpose of deception. The rising of birds in their flight is the sign of an ambuscade. Startled beasts indicate that a sudden attack is forthcoming.

Dust spurting upwards in high straight columns indicates the approach of chariots. When it hangs low and is widespread, it betokens that infantry is approaching. When it branches out in different directions, it shows that parties have been sent out to collect firewood. A few clouds of dust moving to and fro signify that the army is camping.

When the enemy's envoys speak in humble terms, but the army continues preparations, that means it will advance. When their language is strong and the enemy pretentiously drives forward, these may be signs that he will retreat. When light chariots first go out and take positions on the wings, it is a sign that the enemy is forming for battle. When the enemy is not in dire straits but asks for a truce, he must be plotting. When his troops march speedily and parade in formations, he is expecting to fight a decisive battle on a fixed date. When half his force advances and half retreats, he is attempting to decoy you.

When his troops lean on their weapons, they are famished. When drawers of water drink before carrying it to camp, his troops are suffering from thirst. When the enemy sees an advantage but does not advance to seize it, he is fatigued.

When birds gather above his camp sites, they are unoccupied. When at night the enemy's camp is clamorous, it betokens nervousness. If there is disturbance in the camp, the general's authority is weak.

If the banners and flags are shifted about, sedition is afoot. If the officers are angry, it means that men are weary. When the enemy feeds his horses with grain, kills the beasts of burden for food and packs up the utensils used for drawing water, he shows no intention to return to his tents and is determined to fight to the death.

When the general speaks in meek and subservient tone to his subordinates, he has lost the support of his men. Too frequent rewards indicate that the general is at the end of his resources; too frequent punishments indicate that he is in dire distress. If the officers at first treat the men violently and later are fearful of them, it shows supreme lack of intelligence.

When envoys are sent with compliments in their mouths, it is a sign that the enemy wishes for a truce.

When the enemy's troops march up angrily and remain facing yours for a long time, neither joining battle nor withdrawing, the situation demands great vigilance and thorough investigation.

In war, numbers alone confer no advantage. If one does not advance by force recklessly, and is able to concentrate his military power through a correct assessment of the enemy situation and enjoys full support of his men, that would suffice. He who lacks foresight and underestimates his enemy will surely be captured by him.

*Another translator reinforces the importance of the leader's skill in making an estimate of the situation:

There is no necessary advantage in numbers. Do not rush forward rashly, but if you calculate the forces of the enemy and then arrange your own strength accordingly you will win. But those who underrate a foe will certainly finish up as prisoners.

A. L. Sadler

Estimate of the Situation as Used by U.S. Army Officers

1. Mission (assigned or deduced)
2. The Situation and Courses of Action
   a. Considerations Affecting the Courses of Action (other operations, environment, enemy, friendly, etc.)
   b. Anticipated Difficulties
3. Analysis of Courses of Action
4. Comparison of Courses of Action
5. Decision = Commander's Concept or Intent

Questions to Determine Your Position

- What position do we own?
- What position do we want?
- Who do we have to outmaneuver?
- How much resource expenditure and time will it take?
- Can we stick it out?
- Will the results justify the expense?

Questions to Determine Your Opponents' Position

- What position do they own?
- What signals indicate they are changing or strengthening their position?
- What position do they want? (Where are they going?)
- What will be the effect on us if they are successful in their current activities?
- What will be the opportunities for us if they are unsuccessful?

Make an Estimate of the Situation—Manager's Commentary

Carefully observe the situation and attack only where real superiority can be obtained.

Amazon.com grew out of founder Jeff Bezos's personal mission to be in business for himself. His course of action was determined when he learned that books were an $82 billion market and annual growth on the Web was predicted at 2,200 percent. He analyzed the opportunity for innovative computerized marketing and decided that the Seattle area would be a good hi-tech base.[1]

General Paul Cerjan, retired U.S. Army, explains how he uses the steps in conducting the Estimate of the Situation (see facing page) as a great tool for the rapid estimate of any contingency. First, you need to determine the mission. Then you start thinking what course of action you are going to take. Then you work that all the way down until you get to the decision and from that flows the operations order—the specific orders concerning what you want done.

Depending on the circumstances, the Estimate of the Situation can be achieved rapidly or require a more lengthy analysis. We unconsciously make a rapid estimation of the situation in personal interfaces. When issuing written plans, we usually initiate an extended analysis of the situation.

I have observed real differences between the way managers from Western and Eastern civilizations gather information to make an Estimate of the Situation. The Western manager is more likely to do a quick study while the Eastern manager will often do a thorough, lengthy analysis.

There are a variety of readily perceived indicators that can help you estimate the situation. These indicators signal the competitive strategy and vulnerability. The breadth of these signals can be understood from one of Sun Tzu's translators who identified 33 different signs of enemy activity by Sun Tzu in this chapter.

In personal interfaces, these indicators are called body language. Crossed arms indicate opposition. Someone leaning forward and listening indicates intent acceptance. A furrowed brow signals that your proposition is being questioned.

In business situations, the signals are also subtly visible. For example, in publicizing pricing moves, companies are signaling their desire to raise prices to others in the industry—and may reduce prices if competitors reject the signal.

All of these overt signals help the observant manager develop an accurate Estimate of the Situation. While one does not want to overestimate the opponent, it can be disastrous to underestimate.

Discipline Can Build Allegiance—Translation

Sun Tzu continues:

If troops are punished before they have grown attached to you, they will be disobedient. If not obedient, it is difficult to employ them. If troops have become attached to you, but discipline is not enforced, you cannot employ them either. Thus, soldiers must be treated in the first instance with humanity, but kept under control by iron discipline. In this way, the allegiance of soldiers is assured.

If orders are consistently carried out and the troops are strictly supervised, they will be obedient. If orders are never carried out, they will be disobedient. And the smooth implementation of orders reflects harmonious relationship between the commander and his troops.*

*Other translators clarify:

If in training soldiers commands are habitually enforced, the army will be well-disciplined; if not, its discipline will be bad. If a general shows confidence in his men but always insists on his orders being obeyed, the gain will be mutual.

Lionel Giles

If people are instructed in rules that are customary, they will be obedient, but they will not obey those to which they are not accustomed. So if it be demonstrated that the rules are customary and reliable all will be able to co-operate harmoniously.

A. L. Sadler

The Role of Discipline

Colonel Ardant du Picq writes:

What makes the soldier capable of obedience and direction in action, is the sense of discipline. This includes: respect for and confidence in his chiefs; confidence in his comrades and fear of their reproaches if he abandons them in danger; his desire to go where others do without trembling more than they; in a word, the whole of esprit de corps. Organizations only can produce these characteristics. Four men equal a lion.

Discipline Can Build Allegiance—Manager's Commentary

Apply the same standards to everyone.

When home run king Henry Aaron was asked the difference between a good team and a great team, he replied promptly, "discipline." With the discipline should come a warm concern for people.

The ideal leader is best described as one who combines excellence as a task specialist with an equal flair for the human aspects of leadership. He or she understands that it is people rather than techniques that really count. The manager does not have to be liked; however, he or she does not have to be disliked. Being fair and impartial does not mean being impersonal. At times hard decisions must be made. When they are not made, the manager abdicates his authority.

What manager does not have his political favorites, perceived with envy by others less favored? Therein lies a complex problem: These politicians are often perceived as delivering bad information to the boss who, in turn, is perceived as delivering bad orders.

When standards for the performance of each process are established and clearly communicated, then managers can issue praise or criticism based on performance against that standard. The general manager of one of the fine hotels of the world explained to me his reason for having standards: "Maintaining known standards keeps me from playing favorites and being criticized for playing favorites." Although we find a system of standards and measures in manufacturing processes, many other office or service processes operate without clearly defined standards. Too often, where there are no standards, criticism and penalties are imposed at the whim of management. The result is confusion and low morale.

As a manager at Burger King, Herman Cain tells how he set a standard for friendly service with the "Happy B.E.E.'s." The B stood for "Bad moods stay home." The E's signified, "Eye contact with customers. Everyday." This success with motivational discipline earned Cain an increase in business and a promotion up the ladder.[2]

Consistently maintaining high standards creates the environment where discipline is effective and accepted. In these circumstances, morale is high.

Personal discipline is equally important. Until a person learns how to command himself or herself, it is unlikely that command over others will be successful.

10

Terrain

Strategic Rules
Know Your Battlefield
Obey the Laws of Leadership
Fight Only the Battles You Can Win
Know Yourself; Know Your Opponent

Terrain is perhaps one of the most overused words in the translations of Sun Tzu. We will define "terrain" to mean "your area of operations"—either internal or external.

Management by wandering around the "terrain" is essential to success. Managers wander around not *to manage*, but rather so they *can manage*. By spending time at the scene of action, managers get a feel for what's happening now. Since many decisions are made at gut level, this "feel" helps process information so managers can determine a successful course of action based on real knowledge of the situation. Too often, we find decisions being made by smart people who know nothing about the circumstances.

Our bias for what we know can lead to misconceptions about the world around us. As Ralph E. Gomory, president of the Sloan Foundation, said, "We are all taught what is known, but we rarely learn about what is not known; and we almost never learn the unknowable." The point is: There is a lot of information outside of our area of operations. Expanding our knowledge base expands our horizon of possibilities.

Formal input systems for information are essential. However, so are informal systems such as when someone talks with his or her "customer"—the customer being defined as the person who receives your process.

Internally, the person who receives your process is also a customer. Within a company, people are often organized into functional departments, and these departments become competitors. Since we don't talk to competitors, there is no communication. The solution must be to achieve linkage between all processes and align them to deliver value to the ultimate customer. Until we focus all processes on the needs of the customer, the enemy will continue to be "us."

Know Your Battlefield—Translation

Sun Tzu says:

Ground may be classified according to its nature as accessible, entangling, temporizing, constricted, precipitous, and distant.

Ground which both we and the enemy can traverse with equal ease is called accessible. On such ground, he who first takes high sunny positions, and keeps his supply routes unimpeded can fight advantageously. Ground easy to reach but difficult to exit is called entangling. The nature of this ground is such that if the enemy is unprepared and you sally out, you may defeat him. But, if the enemy is prepared for your coming, and you fail to defeat him, then, return being difficult, disadvantages will ensue.

Ground equally disadvantageous for both the enemy and ourselves to enter is called temporizing. This ground is such that even though the enemy offers us an attractive bait, it will be advisable not to go forth but march off. When his force is halfway out because of our maneuvering, we can strike him with advantage. With regard to the constricted ground, if we first occupy it, we must block the narrow passes with strong garrisons and wait for the enemy. If the enemy first occupies such ground, do not attack him if the pass in his hand is fully garrisoned, but only if it is weakly garrisoned.

With regard to the precipitous ground, if we first occupy it, we must take a position on the sunny heights and await the enemy. If he first occupies such ground, we should march off and do not attack him. When the enemy is situated at a great distance from us, and the terrain where the two armies deploy is similar, it is difficult to provoke battle and unprofitable to engage him.

These are the principles relating to six different types of ground. It is the highest responsibility of the general to inquire into them with the utmost care. Conformation of the ground is of great assistance in the military operations. It is necessary for a wise general to make correct assessments of the enemy's situation to create conditions leading to victory and to calculate distances and the degree of difficulty of the terrain. He who knows these things and applies them to fighting will definitely win. He who knows them not, and, therefore, is unable to apply them, will definitely lose.

Know Your Battlefield—Manager's Commentary

Thorough knowledge of the scene of action is an absolute requirement.

If you were fishing in the Southwest some years ago, you might have been approached by two people of Asian descent in a pickup truck offering to clean your rod and reel. They would ask questions about your preferences in fishing equipment. Today, the Japanese are major factors in this business category.

Your "market" is those whom you must persuade to buy your product, service, or idea. The admonition to know your market may seem too basic. However, it is the basics we so often miss. To know your market, you must listen to your customers. To listen effectively, you must ask questions to probe for information. This is "shut up and listen" time. Avoid defensive responses.

The big question is: "What do we need to know to make the required decision?" If we do not know what we need to know, then everything looks like important information. It becomes impossible to sort the useless from the useful.

Often, we are told what someone thinks we want to hear. Just as often, our bias from prior knowledge keeps us from finding the truth. That is why time must be spent at the scene of action finding out what's going on so we know what questions to ask.

Napoleon used both his regular army intelligence system and a focused intelligence telescope of select senior officers to gather information. Senior officers were given wide latitude to report on "anything that might interest me." Junior officers in his regular intelligence system were sent on more specific missions. He deliberately kept his telescope staff small in order to establish personal contact with these messengers. The personal contact helped him evaluate the information he received.

This focused telescope overcomes the common problem of intelligence bureaucracies. Too often, information that gets to the senior commanders is filtered through the chain of command and becomes less and less specific. The result is overgeneralization of information; consequently, those in command know the least about what is really happening. The manager's solution to learning how to interpret data is always to spend time face to face in the battlefield where the data was collected.

Don't shoot the messenger. The most rapid way to shell-shock a business is to shell-proof its managers.

Obey the Laws of Leadership—Translation

Sun Tzu continues:

There are six situations that cause an army to fail. They are: flight, insubordination, fall, collapse, disorganization, and rout. None of these disasters can be attributed to natural and geographical causes, but to the fault of the general.

Terrain conditions being equal, if a force attacks one ten times its size, the result is flight.

When the soldiers are strong and officers weak, the army is insubordinate.

When the officers are valiant and the soldiers ineffective, the army will fall.

When the higher officers are angry and insubordinate, and on encountering the enemy rush to battle on their own account from a feeling of resentment and the commander-in-chief is ignorant of their abilities, the result is collapse.

When the general is incompetent and has little authority, when his troops are mismanaged, when the relationship between the officers and men is strained, and when the troop formations are slovenly, the result is disorganization.

When a general unable to estimate the enemy's strength uses a small force to engage a larger one or weak troops to strike the strong, or fails to select shock troops for the van, the result is riot.

When any of these six situations exists, the army is on the road to defeat. It is the highest responsibility of the general that he examine them carefully.

If a general regards his men as infants, then they will march with him into the deepest valleys. He treats them as his own beloved sons and they will stand by him unto death. If, however, a general is indulgent towards his men but cannot employ them, cherishes them but cannot command them or inflict punishment on them when they violate the regulations, then they may be compared to spoiled children, and are useless for any practical purpose.

Obey the Laws of Leadership—Manager's Commentary

Winning is the responsibility of the leader.

The following characteristics define good command systems:

Decentralization: People have the authority needed to achieve objectives except for that which is expressly forbidden. This reduces the need for detailed control and frees the time of leaders at all levels. Every leader commands his or her own unit; every subordinate knows from where to expect his or her instructions.

Freedom: To generate independence, freedom must be delegated all the way through the chain of command. The system doesn't work when middle managers become infatuated with their own power and fail to give up power as they are given more power in a decentralized command system.

Information Processing: When senior managers give up control, they must also give up some information flow. If not, subordinates will spend too much time reporting to be effective. The task of senior management is not to confirm plans in detail; rather, it is to encourage greater speed.

Stability: People relationships and informal systems give stability to the structure of the command system.

Mutual Trust: The interaction of long-standing relationships creates mutual trust. The replacement system that brings in new personnel should be structured to help create the familiarity that is an indispensable prerequisite of both reliability and trust.

A Willingness to Assume Responsibility: To train people to accept responsibility, authority must be delegated. A decentralized command system leaves much to the discretion of individual commanders and puts responsibility squarely on their shoulders.

The Right and Duty of Subordinate Commanders to Make Decisions and Carry Them Out: Freedom is granted to allow managers to make decisions and utilize available resources to find the best way to the objective.

Expect the Unpredictable: Expect that plans will break down, that your opponent will behave in an unexpected manner, and that units will not achieve their objectives. Don't try to overcome the confusion by pausing to regroup after each breakdown. Keep everyone marching in the right direction.

Training: Every manager manages the training of his or her personnel. This does not mean that he or she conducts all sessions. It does mean that he or she has the basic responsibility for training.[1]

Fight Only the Battles You Can Win—Translation

Sun Tzu continues:

Hence, if, in the light of the prevailing situation, fighting is sure to result in victory, then you may decide to fight* even though the sovereign has issued an order not to engage.

If fighting does not stand a good chance of victory, you need not to fight even though the sovereign has issued an order to engage.

Hence, the general who advances without coveting fame and retreats without fearing disgrace, whose only purpose is to protect his people and promote the best interests of his sovereign, is the precious jewel of the state.

* ... a superior general estimates the enemy situation, calculates distances and difficulty so as to control victory. He who fights with full knowledge of these factors is certain to win.

General Tao Hanzhang

Initiating the Battle

There are two mental approaches to launching the attack:

1. Plan everything in detail and then start going. The battle of the Somme was one of the most thoroughly organized in history. The final deployment of the British attacking force took four months and was a masterpiece of scientific management. Every

unit reached its starting position on time. The result was not victory, but rather one of the worst catastrophes to befall an army in the history of war. The casualties the first day exceeded sixty thousand men.

2. Lay down general objectives only and start immediately. The offensive is launched with the understanding that forward movement will proceed according to local circumstances. The details are filled in as the attack gains momentum. This system is used by the Israeli Defense Force.[2]

It would seem the choice is either to *do it now* or spend time preparing to *do it later*. How difficult it is to achieve the careful balance between getting ready and getting going. The best odds for success lie on the side of action. Most often, the person who does something has the best opportunity to become master of the situation.

Fight Only the Battles You Can Win—Manager's Commentary

First understand the situation, then determine whether to fight and how.

Every executive encounters the decision of where and how to expend energy in two primary areas: the political arena and performance of his or her assigned tasks (either internal or external depending on job function).

The political battles can be the most time consuming and debilitating. The larger the organization, the bigger is the political morass. Halberstam explains one type of dysfunction in his description of conflict at Ford Motor Company in *The Reckoning:*

The growing power of the finance people made the creative people more vulnerable than ever. For the creative people always, no matter how good they were, made mistakes. No product man was perfect; for every model that was a success, there were others best forgotten. By contrast, the finance men were careful. They were never identified with a particular product. They never had to create anything. In meetings they attacked but never had to defend, while the product people defended and could never attack.

In internal politics, while defending your position, target your battle against processes and systems instead of individuals. The person you attack may someday be your boss.

In determining where to fight external battles, keep your orientation focused on effectiveness. Where can you add value and win? The larger the target the bigger will be the results. You cannot be strong everywhere; you must determine where you are going to put your main effort and then exercise the discipline that allocates resources, directly and indirectly, to support this main effort.

If we are not effective, we have no need to be efficient. Ask Ford about its Edsel, Gerber about its failed venture into adult foods, or the corner grocer who went out of business.

Market testing determines whether to launch a full-scale offensive. Your first objective in a test is to determine whether the concept works. Consequently, you must apply full resources to the effort. If the test fails when backed with adequate resources, you know you must abandon the effort. If it succeeds, you can adjust to make it profitable. Half-hearted tests tell you nothing.

We need to be efficient, but not at the expense of the resources needed to achieve success. An inefficient victory is bad, but not as bad as losing—which is extremely inefficient.

Know Yourself; Know Your Opponent—Translation

Sun Tzu says:

   If we know that our troops are capable of striking the enemy, but do not know that he is invulnerable to attack, our chance of victory is but half.

   If we know that the enemy is vulnerable to attack but do not know that our troops are incapable of striking him, our chance of victory is again but half.

If we know that the enemy can be attacked and that our troops are capable of attacking him, but do not realize that the conformation of the ground makes fighting impracticable, our chance of victory is once again but half.

Therefore, when those experienced in war move, they are never bewildered; when they act, they are never at a loss. Thus the saying: *Know the enemy and know yourself, and your victory will never be endangered;* know the weather and know the ground, and your victory will then be complete.

Now, the key to military operations lies in cautiously studying the enemy's designs. Concentrate your forces in the main direction against the enemy and from a distance of a thousand li you can kill his general. This is called the ability to achieve one's aim in an artful and ingenious manner.

*All translations use a similar wording:

Know the enemy and know yourself and you will never be defeated.

Visible and Invisible Numbers

Even when accurate, statistics can never substitute for looking someone in the eye when you get the answer to your question.

Dr. W. Edwards Deming, who championed statistical quality control as a key ingredient of a quality methodology, commented that some managers look only at the visible numbers. He said, " . . . but the visible numbers tell them so little. They know nothing of the invisible numbers. Who can put a price on a satisfied customer and who can figure out the cost of a dissatisfied customer?"

How easy it can be to stroke ourselves with our own convictions and ignore the signals. The process can be a spiral that ends in disaster.

Know Yourself; Know Your Opponent—Manager's Commentary

Know the strengths and weaknesses of your adversary.

When I visited the Philips office in Sao Paulo, Brazil, a senior manager told me that he employed a woman of Japanese descent as a secretary because she could read the Japanese papers ordered from Tokyo. Caterpillar understands this in Peoria because it knows the Peoria paper is delivered daily by air to its competitors in Japan.

Communications are making the world smaller and world competitors better informed. The cost of a three-minute call from New York to London has decreased from over $200 in 1930 to about $2 today. An e-mail sent to anywhere in the world is often at no additional expense because the contact time is part of the monthly fee. The fax has made it possible to send pages of detailed information. For most companies, market research has expanded from domestic to world markets because we can sell to the world and the world can sell anywhere.

There are countless people who call on you who also call on your competitor. The editors of trade magazines know what is going on in the industry. The suppliers who call on purchasing agents know who is buying more and who is buying less—and why. Advertising and promotion agents are another source. So are people who come for job interviews. Beware of the supplier who tells you everything about your competitor because he is also telling your competition about you.

Business executives who change jobs will bring their preferences in methodologies with them. They will usually clone the style of their previous organization. You can predict what they will do by where they have been. Look at both the issues and personalities. Review the issues in terms of history—who did something like this before, what happened. Look at the personalities in terms of their background of experience.

Knowledge of the personal style of competitors is the easy part. Knowledge of one's self is the hard part. The higher the rank, the more difficult it is to get true feedback on one's actions. Don't expect it from anyone internally. The self-examination takes place in three spheres: physical, intellectual, and moral. For physical health, see a doctor; for intellectual health, read, listen, and visit your battlefield; for moral health, find an external guru who will hold up a mirror and give you an honest picture.

11

The Nine Varieties of Ground

Strategic Rules
Choose a Favorable Battleground
Shape Your Opponent's Strategy
Make Victory the Only Option
Plan Coordinated Efforts
Press the Attack
Learn Winning Ways

An ancient proverb says the first blow is as much as two. The attack has the advantage of the initiative. Since it forces action on the opponent, it relegates him or her to second place. The offensive action also strengthens the morale and confidence of the aggressor.

The offensive must be a continuing process. Only then does it permit you to maintain freedom of action, meet unexpected developments, and determine the future courses of action.

Tactical considerations influence strategic plans. That is, you may need to launch your offensive where it is tactically possible, not where it is strategically desirable. For example, a company with a high-end product strategy might determine that competitive success with a specific product in a mid-priced position is more readily attainable.

Two important components of the successful campaign are to strengthen customer value and know your opponent's strengths and weaknesses. In the attack, a fundamental principle is to *avoid that which is strong and attack that which is weak.*

While it is important to do things that give you an advantage, give serious consideration to actions that also put your competitor at a disadvantage.

The concepts of niching and segmentation provide excellent opportunities for maximizing strengths in developing offensive thrusts. Segmentation is a way for anyone of any size to secure a position by focusing strengths on a specific, narrow frontage of the market.

Choose a Favorable Battleground—Translation

Sun Tzu says:

In respect to the employment of troops, ground may be classified as dispersive, frontier, key, open, focal, serious, difficult, encircled, and desperate.

When a chieftain is fighting in his own territory, he is in dispersive ground. When he has penetrated into hostile territory, but to no great distance, he is in frontier ground. Ground equally advantageous for us and the enemy to occupy is key ground. Ground equally accessible to both sides is open. Ground contiguous to three other states is focal. He who first gets control of it will gain the support of the majority of neighboring states. When an army has penetrated deep into hostile territory, leaving far behind many enemy cities and towns, it is in serious ground. Mountain forests, rugged steeps, marshes, fens, and all that is hard to traverse fall into the category of difficult ground. Ground to which access is constricted and from which we can only retire by tortuous paths so that a small number of the enemy would suffice to crush a large body of our men is encircled ground. Ground on which the army can avoid annihilation only through a desperate fight without delay is called a desperate one.

And, therefore, do not fight in dispersive ground; do not stop in the frontier borderlands.

Do not attack an enemy who has occupied key ground; in open ground, do not allow your communication to be blocked.

In focal ground, form alliances with neighboring states; in serious ground, gather in plunder.

In difficult ground, press on; in encircled ground, resort to stratagems; and in desperate ground, fight courageously.

The principle of terrain application is to make the best use of both the high and the low-lying grounds. *

*Samuel B. Griffith translates:

The tactical variations appropriate to the nine types of ground, the advantages of close or extended deployment, and the principles of human nature are matters the general must examine with the greatest care.

Choose a Favorable Battleground—Manager's Commentary

Control of the location of the battleground results in control of offensive and defensive actions.

Continental Airlines president Gordon Bethune found it cost more money to have problems of planes being late or dirty or needing maintenance than to solve these problems. In a survey of customers, Continental found that nothing else scored as high in importance as having planes on time. As a result, on-time performance was chosen as the battleground and major metric. Continental established a program to reward employees for on-time performance. Soon, Continental was rated first in on-time arrivals.

Although planes were arriving on time, baggage wasn't, so Continental expanded the reward system to include performance in the entire system. Soon, everyone understood that his or her primary job focus was to run a good airline.[1]

To discover new marketing battlefields, Pfizer organized its drug-discovery teams to pursue development of drugs for every major disease. It built speed into the process so that its drug-discovery teams needed less than one-third the industry's average person-years to move a compound from conception to clinical trials. When Pfizer researchers found themselves in a race with a Japanese company for an Alzheimer's drug similar to theirs, they opted to drop research and form a more favorable joint venture so they could co-market the drug.

Twenty-five thousand new products are launched every year. The average forecast is that one in several hundred will succeed. Research, targeting, and luck are critical to determining where resources should be invested.

Big Island Candy in Hilo, Hawaii, selected a unique battlefield that avoids retail distribution where its product would compete with the bigger mass-marketed brands. Instead, the focus is on the tour operators who are pleased that the visit to the Big Island Candy store and factory offers branded products that are not available in retail stores at a discount. This marketing approach is quite immune to the moves of big competitors.

The most favorable battleground is always where you can concentrate your resources profitably with minimal competition. To control the battleground, you must offer a distinctive differentiation and the customer must desire that differentiation. Otherwise, you are another player in a low-margin commodity market.

Shape Your Opponent's Strategy—Translation

Sun Tzu continues:

In ancient times, those described as skilled in war knew how to make it impossible for the enemy to unite his van and his rear, for his large and small divisions to cooperate, for his officers and men to support each other, and for the higher and lower levels of the enemy to establish contact with each other.

When the enemy's forces were dispersed, they prevented him from assembling them; even when assembled, they managed to throw his forces into disorder. They moved forward when it was advantageous to do so; when not advantageous, they halted.

Should one ask: "How do I cope with a well-ordered enemy host about to attack me?" I reply, "Seize something he cherishes and he will conform to your desires."

Speed is the essence of war. Take advantage of the enemy's unpreparedness, make your way by unexpected routes, and attack him where he has taken no precautions.*

*Other translators' interpretations of how your attack can shape the opponent's strategy:

In the conduct of war, speed is everything. Take the enemy unawares, follow the route unthought of by him and attack the place left ungarrisoned by him.

Zhang Huimin

It is the nature of the army to stress speed; to take advantage of the enemy's absence; to travel unanticipated roads; and to attack when they are not alert.

Ralph D. Sawyer

Rapidity is the essence of war; take advantage of the enemy's unreadiness, make your way by unexpected routes, and attack unguarded spots.

Lionel Giles

Shape Your Opponent's Strategy—Manager's Commentary

Move swiftly to disrupt your opponent and place him at the disadvantage.

Seventy-five percent of men between ages eighteen and forty-five own at least one pair of Dockers. Campbell's owns 75 percent of the condensed soup business. A company called Play-by-Play dominates the $190 million carnival-prize market with a 50 percent share.[2] These giants determine the marketing situation in their industries. They own the market, and their opponents must shape their attack around the strategies of these giants because the gorilla sleeps anywhere he wants.

Whether or not you can shape your opponent's strategy in business situations is a function of your relative strength. Although this relative strength is most often seen in established gorillas, new entrants with a differentiation who move rapidly can become powerful gorillas. Witness the rapid rise of Amazon.com in Web marketing, TCBY in yogurt, and Staples in office products. These organizations matched differentiation with speed in order to attain strength.

Pepsi was big enough to be a threat to Coke when Pepsi launched its blind taste test campaign to prove that more people preferred the flavor of Pepsi. Coke responded by launching a new formula and renaming the original product Coke Classic. However, the market responded negatively to the new Coke, and Pepsi's attempt to reshape Coke's strategy had only a temporary effect.

You can force your opponent to react when you rapidly accumulate a critical mass of power. Napoleon said, "Force must be concentrated at one point and as soon as the breach is made, the equilibrium is broken."

In 1914, Captain Johnstone wrote that full strength is recognized as a key principle in shaping success. He says, "The best thing is to have as much as you can for yourself and as little as you can for the enemy." It is strength at a given point that shapes the opponent's reaction.

In every competitive endeavor, a concentration of energy must be rapidly achieved to attain the breakthrough. The winning manager must give priority to those items that are the most critical to success. The ultimate judge of whether you win is the customer. His or her decision to buy is the critical vote. If the customer doesn't vote with a favorable decision, nothing else matters.

Make Victory the Only Option—Translation

Sun Tzu continues:

Throw your soldiers into a position whence there is no escape, and they will choose death over desertion. For if prepared to die, how can the officers and men not exert their uttermost strength to fight? In a desperate situation, they fear nothing; when there is no way out, they stand firm. Deep in a hostile land they are bound together. If there is no help for it, they will fight hard.

Thus, without waiting to be marshaled, the soldiers will be constantly vigilant; without waiting to be asked, they will do your will; without restrictions, they will be faithful; without giving orders, they can be trusted.

Prohibit superstitious practices and do away with rumors, then nobody will flee even facing death. Our soldiers have no surplus of wealth, but it is not because they disdain riches; they have no expectation of long life, but it is not because they dislike longevity.

On the day the army is ordered out to battle, your soldiers may weep, those sitting up wetting their garments, and those lying down letting the tears run down their cheeks. But throw them into a situation where there is no escape and they will display the immortal courage of Zhuan Zhu and Cao Kuei.

He orders his troops for a decisive battle on a fixed date and cuts off their return route, as if he kicks away the ladder behind the soldiers when they have climbed up a height. When he leads his army deep into hostile territory, their momentum is trigger-released in battle. He drives his men now in one direction, then in another, like a shepherd driving a flock of sheep, and no one knows where he is going. To assemble the host of his army and bring it into danger—this may be termed the business of the general.

Set the troops to their tasks without revealing your designs. When the task is dangerous, do not tell them its advantageous aspect. Throw them into a perilous situation and they will survive; put them in desperate ground and they will live. For when the army is placed in such a situation, it can snatch victory from defeat.

Make Victory the Only Option—Manager's Commentary

Lead your forces into situations where they cannot retreat.

Underlying Sun Tzu's comments is the idea that the need to survive can do much to rally everyone to achieve goals. The pressure here is of two types: personal or corporate survival.

> *Corporate Survival:* We have seen dramatic success from a common understanding of the need for corporate survival. This was particularly true during the early days of the quality revolution when higher quality imports threatened lower quality domestic products. Then the rallying cry was to improve quality in order to stay in business.
>
> *Personal Survival:* The threat of either getting your job done right or losing it has been used by aggressive management at all levels. At companies like Pepsi, it has historically been common knowledge among managers that you make your numbers or you leave.

Competition for personal survival is also keen at the real-world management schools within corporate America such as Procter & Gamble, General Electric, and Disney. Although renowned as training grounds for leaders, the survival process ranges from tough to brutal. The Disney system pits strong division managers against a strategic planning group that acts as a check on their power. Conflict is inherent in this system. To survive, you must fly under the radar as long as possible.[3]

Each individual must build the kind of career strength that makes him or her marketable. Says Intel's Andrew Grove, "No matter where you work, you are not an employee. You are in a business with one employer—yourself—in competition with millions of similar businesses worldwide. . . . Nobody owes you a career—you own it as a sole proprietor. And the key to survival is to learn to add more value every day."[4]

With each job change or promotion, you increase your career knowledge and your value to the next employer. If you aren't moving up in your organization, then consider moving on.

In hiring people, I have always been impressed when the background indicates that one of the prior employers had a reputation for thorough screening of new hires. After selection comes training. If your company isn't training you, then you should be sending yourself to training—and that includes training inside and outside your profession.

Plan Coordinated Efforts—Translation

Sun Tzu continues:

Troops directed by a skillful general are comparable to the Shuai Ran. The Shuai Ran is a snake found in Mount Heng. Strike at its head, and you will be attacked by its tail; strike at its tail, and you will be attacked by its head; strike at its middle, and you will be attacked by both its head and its tail. Should one ask: "Can troops be made capable of such instantaneous coordination as the Shuai Ran?" I reply, "They can." For the men of Wu and the men of Yue are enemies, yet if they are crossing a river in the same boat and are caught by a storm, they will come to each other's assistance just as the left hand helps the right.

Hence, it is not sufficient to rely upon tethering of the horses and the burying of the chariots. The principle of military administration is to achieve a uniform level of courage.

Thus, a skillful general conducts his army just as if he were leading a single man, willy-nilly, by the hand.

The general principles applicable to an invading force are that the deeper you penetrate into hostile territory, the greater will be the solidarity of your troops, and thus the defenders cannot overcome you.

Teamwork Works

Colonel Ardant du Picq crystallized the fundamental principle underlying teamwork: "Four brave men who do not know each other well will not dare attack a lion. Four less brave, but knowing each other well, sure of their reliability and consequently of mutual aid, will attack resolutely. There is the science of organization of armies in a nutshell."

And there is the science of organization for *teamwork* in a nutshell!

Colonel du Picq continues, "At any time a new invention may assure victory. Granted. But practicable weapons are not invented every day . . . the determining factor, leaving aside generals of genius, and luck, is the quality of troops, that is, the organization that best assures their esprit, their reliability, their confidence, their unity."[5]

Plan Coordinated Efforts—Manager's Commentary

A united effort has strength.

There are many different ways to coordinate efforts. Coca-Cola has focused on making its worldwide bottling operations more cohesive by building its strength around its larger, stronger partners.

Acquisition is another approach to obtaining a stronger united effort. The most effective acquisitions are "bolt ons" to existing core strengths. Acquiring diverse, small companies to build a conglomerate is usually not an effective strategy.

Taking an internally focused approach to coordinated efforts, Tenneco has transformed from a highly diversified conglomerate into a focused global manufacturer of parts and packaging.

Dana's reorganization took a different tack as it divided into six strategic business units to allow each to focus strength on a segment.

Successful companies spend a lot of time forming small teams with the mobility to maneuver. Five-billion-dollar giant Illinois Tool Works operates through 365 small, decentralized business units that actively practice teamwork with customers and suppliers. Some may think it is inefficient to break the unit into small groups. So is defeat.

Two-time Baldrige winner Solectron is just one of many who have saved billions of dollars with teams focused on process improvement. To achieve this kind of savings, organizations have invested in training people in quality management and teamwork skills. Trained team facilitators are used to enhance team performance.

Forming effective teams takes time and training. The most successful teams are those with the best training and leadership. Successful strategic decisions are most likely to be made by teams that promote active and broad conflict over issues without sacrificing speed. The key to doing so is to mitigate interpersonal conflict. Too often, the absence of conflict is not harmony, it's apathy.[6]

When people are empowered and trained to work effectively in teams, they take ownership of the task; and the entire management process moves from control to commitment.

The team structure must be cascaded throughout the organization. Teamwork works only when it is led from the top. When the senior management staff functions as a team, then the stage is set for all other units to operate as teams.

Press the Attack—Translation

Sun Tzu continues:

Plunder fertile country to supply your army with plentiful food. Pay attention to the soldiers' well-being and do not fatigue them. Try to keep them in high spirits and conserve their energy. Keep the army moving and devise unfathomable plans.

It is the business of a general to be quiet and thus ensure depth in deliberation; impartial and upright, and thus keep a good management.

He should be able to mystify his officers and men by false reports and appearances, and thus keep them in total ignorance. He changes his arrangements and alters his plans in order to make others unable to see through his strategies. He shifts his campsites and undertakes marches by devious routes so as to make it impossible for others to anticipate his objective.

The different measures appropriate to the nine varieties of ground and the expediency of advance or withdrawal in accordance with circumstances and the fundamental laws of human nature are matters that must be studied carefully by a general.

Generally, when invading a hostile territory, the deeper the troops penetrate, the more cohesive they will be; penetrating only a short way causes dispersion.

When you leave your own country behind, and take your army across neighboring territory, you find yourself on critical ground.

When there are means of communication on all four sides, it is focal ground.

When you penetrate deeply into a country, it is serious ground.

When you penetrate but a little way, it is frontier ground.

When you have the enemy's strongholds on your rear, and narrow passes in front, it is encircled ground. When there is no place of refuge at all, it is desperate ground.

Press the Attack—Manager's Commentary

Keep the pressure on.

The success of organizations like Southwest Airlines and Nordstrom was not achieved with a single thrust; instead, they kept pressing the attack as they invaded each successive market.

Southwest Airlines developed systems for turning around planes faster and having crews perform multiple tasks. It kept costs low and innovated low-priced fare structures. Today, there are only two kinds of airports: those served by Southwest and those who wish they were on a Southwest route.

Nordstrom developed a customer service philosophy and high-end brand presentation that has made it the envy of the department store industry. In an industry where it is difficult to find a clerk to take your money, Nordstrom made customer service a hallmark. While new discount stores flourish with low-end products, Nordstrom continues its offensive of high-quality and value merchandise.

Several key ingredients are common to all growing organizations:

Customer Focus: It matters not whether you are in a high-end business category like Nordstrom or more value oriented like Southwest; both are rated high by customers because they have created systems that deliver perceived value.

Selection: The most important contributor to the success of any organization is the ability to hire good people. I spent hours interviewing Phillip Fulmer, head football coach at the University of Tennessee, as I assisted with his book *Legacy of Winning.* Fulmer has one of the top winning records in college football and as such can attract good people. However, he doesn't sit around waiting for them to knock on the door; he has a well-organized, systematic campaign to analyze candidates and encourage the best to sign up on his team—and so does Microsoft.

Training: Hiring good people alone is not enough. Whether coaching a sports team or leading a business venture, you must be able to train the unit to be the very best. Extensive training on an ongoing basis is the hallmark of premier organizations, where learning sessions are highly interactive.

The pressure necessary for success is applied by good people working within good systems that empower them to use their skills.

Learn Winning Ways—Translation

Sun Tzu continues:
    Therefore, in dispersive ground, I would unify the determination of the army. In frontier ground, I would keep my forces closely linked. In key ground, I would hasten up my rear elements. In open ground, I would pay close attention to my defense. In focal ground, I would

consolidate my alliances. In serious ground, I would ensure a continuous flow of provisions. In difficult ground, I would press on over the road. In encircled ground, I would block the points of access and egress. In desperate ground, I would make it evident that there is no chance of survival. For it is the nature of soldiers to resist when surrounded, to fight hard when there is no alternative, and to follow commands implicitly when they have fallen into danger.

One ignorant of the designs of neighboring states cannot enter into alliance with them; if ignorant of the conditions of mountains, forests, dangerous defiles, swamps, and marshes, he cannot conduct the march of an army; if he fails to make use of native guides, he cannot gain the advantages of the ground.

An army does not deserve the title of the invincible Army of the Hegemonic King if its commander is ignorant of even one of these nine varieties of ground. Now, when such an invincible army attacks a powerful state, it makes it impossible for the enemy to assemble his forces. It overawes the enemy and prevents his allies from joining him. It follows that one does not need to seek alliances with other neighboring states, nor is there any need to foster the power of other states, but only to *pursue one's own strategic designs to overawe his enemy. Then one can take the enemy's cities and overthrow the enemy's state.**

Bestow rewards irrespective of customary practice and issue orders irrespective of convention and you can command a whole army as though it were but one man.

*Roger Ames translates:

If you pursue your own program, and bring your prestige and influence to bear on the enemy, you can take his walled cities and lay waste to his state.

Learn Winning Ways—Manager's Commentary

Problems are opportunities.

Winning companies are always on the offensive: Dell with new products and new markets overseas, Nucor Steel with the lowest labor cost per ton, and Wal-Mart with its ever expanding international network of new stores.

Here are a few fundamental characteristics of winners:

Fight the Battles That Count: While you should not fight political battles you cannot win, when you win political battles and make enemies, you run the risk of becoming weaker. In too many cases, qualified, active people are not promoted because they have made enemies. When you can win and retain good relationships, only then can you become strong.

Avoid the Avoidable: The process of avoiding the avoidable is understanding that physical hazards are identifiable obstacles against which specific measures can be taken. In contrast, the human element is completely unpredictable. Take specific actions to reduce the possibility of defeat as a result of physical conditions. This lets you devote full resources to dealing with unpredictable human elements.

Every document you present has both form and substance. You must go for the ultimate quality in the physical element of form so it doesn't detract from the more psychological elements of substance.

Considering the fragility of the human element, leave all possibilities for controllable physical mistakes to your opponent and organize for minimum physical defects in your operation. Do not allow your plan to fail because of the quality of the product, or the delivery time, or any physical element. The organization for excellence does not require that headquarters assumes control of everything—often decentralization is the best way to avoid physical problems.

Communicate Expectations; Reward Achievements: Everyone must understand performance expectations in terms of specific, identifiable goals and rewards. People respond in relation to the way they are measured and rewarded.

Use a written charter to assign tasks to a team and establish boundaries. The team develops a mission statement and reconciles it with the chartering authority. Hold a celebration when results are achieved.

Set High Goals: The way to consistently hit your target is to plan to achieve beyond the target. Then when you fall short, you will probably hit your goal.

12

Attack by Fire

Strategic Rules
Be Disruptive and Intrusive
Consolidate Your Gains
Exercise Restraint

People who concentrate all of their efforts on tactical issues only are working short term. They will eventually be overwhelmed by those who are doing the right thing today as part of a longer-term strategic plan. We can find the overemphasis on tactics in those who work in the more tactical selling and advertising areas of business. The overly tactical salesperson is characterized as one who concentrates only on the immediate sale and not on the long-term selling and service relationship with the customer. Overly tactical advertising concentrates on low prices without considering the debilitating effects of too much price advertising. There's an admonition: "People don't buy price; they are sold price."

The right long-term strategy can be in conflict with the need for immediate results. While a particular strategic approach may appear conceptually sound, the organization may deplete its resources before the plan yields results.

Battles can be won with tactics; however, long-range business victory comes only with the proper balance of strategy and tactics. Strategic results can be achieved only with the right mix of thinking and doing.

The offensive military commander has always known that breakthroughs are opportunities which must be exploited. Somehow this simple truth often gets lost in the bureaucracy of organizations.

For organizations to change, the culture must change. One of the most difficult tasks facing managers who want to initiate change is how to overcome the ghosts of past corporate cultures. Even when senior managers let go of control and try to decentralize, they find scores of subordinates patiently waiting for instructions or authority. Leaders who want to reshape organizational culture must continually and actively reinforce the messages they want to deliver.

Be Disruptive and Intrusive—Translation

Sun Tzu says:

There are five ways of attacking with fire. The first is to burn soldiers in their camp; the second, to burn provision and stores; the third, to burn baggage-trains; the fourth, to burn arsenals and magazines; and the fifth, to burn the lines of transportation.

To use fire, some medium must be relied upon. Materials for setting fire must always be at hand. There are suitable seasons to attack with fire, and special days for starting a conflagration. The suitable seasons are when the weather is very dry; the special days are those when the moon is in the constellations of the Sieve, the Wall, the Wing or the Cross-bar; for when the moon is in these positions there are likely to be strong winds all day long.

Now, in attacking with fire, one must respond to the five changing situations: When fire breaks out in the enemy's camp, immediately coordinate your action from without. If there is an outbreak of fire, but the enemy's soldiers remain calm, bide your time and do not attack. When the force of the flames has reached its height, follow it up with an attack, if that is practicable; if not, stay where you are. If fires can be raised from outside the enemy's camps, it is not necessary to wait until they are started inside. Attack with fire only when the moment is suitable. If the fire starts from up-wind, do not launch attack from down-wind. When the wind continues blowing during the day, then it is likely to die down at night.

Now, the army must know the five different fire-attack situations and wait for appropriate times.

Those who use fire to assist their attacks can achieve tangible results; those who use inundations can make their attacks more powerful.* Water can intercept and isolate an enemy, but cannot deprive him of the supplies or equipment.

*Thomas Cleary translates:

The use of fire to help an attack means clarity; the use of water to help an attack means strength.

Be Disruptive and Intrusive—Manager's Commentary

Disrupt the mind and intrude into that disruption.

During the Olympics, the Swatch Watch brand gained attention with a giant watch replica hanging on the side of a building. When I wanted to emphasize a profit opportunity in software, I arranged for $1 million in one-dollar bills to be stacked in a giant 20-foot high display at a trade show. When Federal Express wanted to dramatize its new Saturday service, it sent thirty thousand coffee cakes to Federal Express customers—delivered by Federal Express, of course.

Every commander in battle strives to achieve the breakthrough. In business, too often the search is confined to the need for sheer numbers to achieve the breakthrough. As we increase our efforts, so do our opponents. After each failure to achieve the breakthrough, the reaction is to call for a little more effort.

When we wish for just a little more time, more funds, more prospects, or more customers, we fail to realize that "just a little more" is not enough. While one company may be planning for just a little more, a competitor may be focusing on achieving a lot more. Guess who wins? Expect unexpected competition and organize for extraordinary achievements.

When we are successful in the attack, it is because of a carefully planned, extraordinary effort. Military leaders say that in order to achieve a breakthrough, two major events must happen:

1. Dislocation: You cannot hit the enemy unless you have first created the opportunity.
2. Exploitation: You cannot make that effect decisive unless you exploit the opportunity before he can recover.

The business equivalent to dislocation and exploitation is to be "disruptive" and "intrusive." You must "disrupt" the mind and "intrude" into that disruption.

Disruptive and intrusive communications have been achieved in a variety of ways. The activity ranges from the unexpected appearance of the boss at an employee event to the publicity stunt that achieves worldwide coverage.

Neither the disruption nor the intrusion that creates attention should be crass or offensive. If the disruption puts people in a negative frame of mind, the strategy backfires. To be effective, the intrusion must be directly related to your message.

Consolidate Your Gains—Translation

Sun Tzu continues:

Now, to win battles and capture lands and cities but to fail to consolidate these achievements is ominous and may be described as a waste of resources and time. And, therefore, the enlightened rulers must deliberate upon the plans to go to battle, and good generals carefully execute them.*

*Here are different interpretations of Sun Tzu's words:

Unhappy is the fate of one who tries to win his battles and succeed in his attacks without cultivating the spirit of enterprise: for the result is a waste of time and general stagnation. Hence the saying: The enlightened ruler lays his plans well ahead; the good general cultivates his resources.

James Clavell

When battles gain victories and attacks achieve occupations, yet these successes are not followed up, it is disastrous. This is known as "persisting turmoil." So an enlightened lord considers these and distinguished commanders follow them.

J. H. Huang

Consolidate Your Gains—Manager's Commentary

Develop sustainable loyalty.

Your objective is not just to win; your objective must be to sustain victory. When the values of the organization focus on rewarding and motivating all stakeholders, continued victory is assured.

Make the sale and lose the customer and you lose the war. In any endeavor, the highest cost is the first sale. Earning that sale is only the basis for future relationships.

The sales manager of one of the world's largest container manufacturers told me he could attribute 58 percent of his business to long-term partnering arrangements. In each instance his company served as the sole or primary supplier to the customer. Business partnerships between customers and suppliers have become an excellent way to convert a series of transactions into a lasting relationship.

Loyalty programs that reward repeat customers are another way to develop continuing relationships. Winning is not achieved in completing one transaction; victory is in the value of multiple purchases over time. Customer loyalty is earned by those organizations who "delight" the customer. That is, these companies do not just make a sale; they satisfy the customer in such an overwhelming manner that a long-term relationship is established. Customers who find the product or service to be outstanding can generate an incredible amount of repeat business. Considerable evidence exists that repeat customers spend more money and are more profitable. The lifelong value of a customer at a gas station accumulates into revenue of tens of thousands of dollars and at an automobile dealership into hundreds of thousands of dollars.

Equally important to customer loyalty is employee loyalty. At Hewlett-Packard when Lewis Platt's wife died, he was thrust into the role of a single parent. When Platt reached the chief executive's position, he found that women employees were leaving in droves. Platt developed a new workplace strategy that actively encouraged employees to adjust their workweeks to meet personal responsibilities. In a memo to employees, Platt stated, "Attention to work/life issues strengthens HP's competitive edge and improves teamwork." When Platt moved up to chairman, his replacement became the third woman to head a Fortune 500 company. Today, Hewlett-Packard's turnover is 5 percent in an industry where the average rate is 17 percent.[1]

Exercise Restraint—Translation

Sun Tzu continues:

If not in the interests of the state, do not act. If you are not sure of success, do not use troops. If you are not in danger, do not fight a battle.*

A sovereign should not launch a war simply out of anger, nor should a general fight a war simply out of resentment. Take action if it is to your advantage; cancel the action if it is not. An angered man can be happy again, just as a resentful one can feel pleased again, but a state that has perished can never revive, nor can a dead man be brought back to life.

Therefore, with regard to the matter of war, the enlightened ruler is prudent, and the good general is full of caution. Thus, the state is kept secure and the army preserved.

*Other translators' interpretations of restraint apply equally to external strategies and internal politics:

Move only when it benefits you. In war you must win; in attacking, you must succeed. If it is not beneficial to the country, do not take action. If you cannot win, do not go to war. If you are not in danger, do not fight.

Brian Bruya

If it is not advantageous, do not move. If objectives cannot be attained, do not employ the army. Unless endangered, do not engage in warfare.

Roger Ames

No action should be taken unless it is to your advantage; no army should be committed unless you are sure of victory; no war should be waged unless you have no alternative.

Zhang Huimin

Exercise Restraint—Manager's Commentary

Do not fight battles you cannot win—or win those that lose the war.

External Restraint

Manufacturers who want to invade new foreign markets have not been very successful with the head-on attack of heavy advertising investments and massive campaigns. New markets are conquered by deliberate, skillfully executed campaigns focused on methodically outmaneuvering entrenched competitors.

Today, Coke has a large share of the Japanese market for soft drinks because it took the time and made the investment to build a full range of functional strengths. When Coke made its first move into Japan, it found a complex, multilayered distribution system. Using local bottlers, Coke recreated the kind of sales force it uses in the United States. Instead of servicing accounts with independent wholesalers or distributors, in Japan today the Coke van replaces empty bottles with new ones. By investing heavily in resources in the distribution system, Coke redefined the domestic game in Japan. Short-term financial returns were sacrificed to achieve long-term gains.[2]

A different approach in the invasion of markets is to use existing distributors and/or sales representatives as the delivery system. Only after strength is achieved is the transition made to corporate distribution centers by either purchasing distribution facilities or buying out agreements. The growth of successful distribution in many industries nationally can be traced from the use of outside agents to internally controlled delivery systems.

Internal Restraint

The issue of fighting a battle you cannot win has special applications for corporate politics. Good politicians negotiate. Bad politicians fight battles.

Hundreds of years before Christ, a Chinese warlord gave the following advice that has real application for corporate politics:

> *One who gains one victory becomes the Emperor;*
> *One who gains two, a King;*
> *One who gains three, Lord Protector;*
> *One who gains four is exhausted;*
> *One who gains five victories suffers calamity.*

13

Employment of Secret Agents

Strategic Rules
Invest in Intelligence Resources
Establish an Active Intelligence System
Practice Counterintelligence

In many organizations, a major problem is organizing, synthesizing, and disseminating information. Most organizations are plagued with "islands of information." Many people know many things, but no system exists to put it all together for verification and application to specific objectives. Even in the CIA, most of the information is obtained from overt, not covert, sources. The biggest job for any intelligence unit is organizing and interpreting readily available information.

Uncertainty surrounds many of the issues which challenge the manager. The antidote for uncertainty is more relevant information. The more information available, the longer the time needed to process it and the greater the danger of failing to distinguish between the relevant and the irrelevant.

According to General Gordon R. Sullivan, the army's recently retired chief of staff, "The paradox of war in the Information Age is one of managing massive amounts of information and resisting the temptation to over-control it. The competitive advantage is nullified when you try to run decisions up and down the chain of command. . . . Once the commander's intent is understood, decisions must be devolved to the lowest possible level to allow these front line soldiers to exploit the opportunities that develop."[1]

Wegmans Food Markets, headquartered in upstate New York, has been described in the *Wall Street Journal* as a retailer somewhere between Nordstrom and Harrods. Wegmans' store managers regularly hold focus group sessions with eight to ten customers to discuss their likes and dislikes. Because this front line research is conducted by store managers with their own customers, suggestions can be immediately implemented. This is just one reason why Wegmans' average store volume is four times greater than the national average.

Invest in Intelligence Resources—Translation

Sun Tzu says:

Generally, when an army of one hundred thousand is raised and dispatched on a distant war, the expenses borne by the people together with the disbursements made by the treasury will amount to a thousand pieces of gold per day. There will be continuous commotion both at home and abroad; people will be involved with convoys and exhausted from performing transportation services, and seven hundred thousand households will be unable to continue their farmwork.

Hostile armies confront each other for years in order to struggle for victory in a decisive battle; *yet if one who begrudges the expenditure of one-hundred pieces of gold in honors and emoluments remains ignorant of his enemy's situation, he is completely devoid of humanity.** Such a man is no leader of the troops; no capable assistant to his sovereign; no master of victory.

*General Tao Hanzhang translates:

If one who begrudges rank, honors, and a few hundred pieces of gold remains ignorant of his enemy's situation, he is completely unaware of the interest of the state and people.

Collect All Available Data

The first rule of data collection is stated in the army regulations of the People's Republic of China:

> *Every commander must organize reconnaissance within his unit's zone of activities. He must not wait for instructions from his superior, nor must he seek his superior's decision as to whether he should organize reconnaissance.*

The second rule of data collection is that much of what you need to know is already known. To learn what needs to be done, search your neighborhood or benchmark the world, and you will find someone who is already doing "it" successfully. Theodore Levitt says it this way: "The future doesn't descend on us on some prophetic day . . . it grows out of forces which are now turbulently in motion."

Invest in Intelligence Resources—Manager's Commentary

Information is crucial to winning.

Successful ventures do good intelligence homework so they can target their products.

Accurate intelligence allows for better use of your resources. The information derived reduces risks because you have the data that gives you better odds. Only a gambler with inside information can rationally bet his or her whole stake on a single race. Good marketing research management puts you in the business of managing risks instead of taking risks.

The key assumption of intelligence is that an impression of what is not known can be pieced together by studying what is known. Good strategy needs good assumptions, and good assumptions are a product of good intelligence.

America's most successful corporations have large cadres of internal and external market research services. They treat marketing research as a corporate asset because it helps them market more effectively and efficiently.

It is easy to do bad market research, because we so often want to ask the questions that will tell us what we want to hear. Before determining questions, you must learn everything you can about the area you want to study. That means personal visits to the places where your product or service is consumed.

Too often, we think that knowledge of ourselves and our opponent is a destination we've already reached. Gathering knowledge is an ongoing, dynamic, feedback process.

Improper action from advance signals can exacerbate the problem. An abundance of information incorrectly interpreted can lead to fatally wrong conclusions.

In intelligence failures, the problem is not that the information is unavailable; rather, it is not taken seriously by commanders who, once committed to a course of action based on bureaucratic consensus, refuse to recognize the validity of contrary data and are unwilling to abandon the original operation.

You must know your opponent and understand his or her strengths and weaknesses. You must understand everything you can about the current and future markets for your product, service, or idea.

Establish an Active Intelligence System—Translation

Sun Tzu continues:

Now, the reason that the enlightened sovereign and the wise general conquer the enemy whenever they move and their achievements surpass those of ordinary men is that they have foreknowledge. This 'foreknowledge' cannot be elicited from spirits, nor from gods, nor by analogy with past events, nor by any deductive calculations. It must be obtained from the men who know the enemy situation.

Hence, the use of spies, of whom there are five sorts: native spies, internal spies, converted spies, doomed spies, and surviving spies.

When all these five sorts of spies are at work and none knows their method of operation, it would be divinely intricate and constitutes the greatest treasure of a sovereign.

Native spies are those we employ from the enemy's country people. Internal spies are enemy officials whom we employ.

Converted spies are enemy spies whom we employ.

Doomed spies are those of our own spies who are deliberately given false information and told to report it.

Surviving spies are those who return from the enemy camp to report information.

Hence, of all those in the army close to the commander, none is more intimate than the spies; of all rewards, none more liberal than those given to spies; of all matters, none is more confidential than those relating to spying operations.

He who is not sage cannot use spies. He who is not humane and generous cannot use spies. And he who is not delicate and subtle cannot get the truth out of them. Delicate indeed! Truly delicate!*

*Another translator identifies the need for the manager's wisdom in conducting research and intelligence activities:

No one but a sage can utilize espionage; except with humanity, one cannot deploy agents; except with thorough observation, one cannot gain truth from agents. Observe! Observe!

J. H. Huang

Establish an Active Intelligence System—Manager's Commentary

Establish a methodology for processing information.

Organize Your Information Flow

The process of gathering intelligence is one of collecting and filtering. All information is not useful. Too much information can make it difficult to separate the useful from the useless. One of the key decisions in processing information is how to be selective in the information flow to each level of management.

The ultimate solution is a combination of:

- Structure, which sizes the organization's decision making process;
- Good information available at all levels;
- Personal reconnaissance on the part of decision makers at every level.

Make Information Useful

To make scattered information useful, it has to be pulled together piece by piece and developed to form distinct patterns to enlighten all echelons. This coordinating process is what makes intelligence useful. Confronted with a task and not having enough information to perform the task, an organization will either centralize or decentralize.

Centralizing keeps decision thresholds high and increases the information flow. Centralization also requires more information processing capability, thereby creating a more complex system.

Decentralizing divides the task into parts and establishes focal points to deal with each part. This relocates the decision thresholds to lower levels.[2]

Most often, the best choice will be to decentralize and segment the task into manageable parts. This requires management that is willing to accept less certainty at the top in order to have more certainty at the bottom.

Systems Are Not Solutions

Too often, managers are disappointed because they expected the new information system to provide new solutions. Battles are not won with systems; they are won with that supreme weapon—the personal factor.

Although it would seem that the command structure should determine whether the information system should be centralized or decentralized, often the reverse is true. It is the ability of the system to absorb and process information that determines whether a centralized or decentralized command structure can be the most effective way to organize.

Practice Counterintelligence—Translation

Sun Tzu continues:

There is no place where espionage is not possible. * If plans relating to spying operations are prematurely divulged, the spy and all those to whom he spoke of them should be put to death.

Generally, whether it be armies that you wish to strike, cities that you wish to attack, and individuals that you wish to assassinate, it is necessary to find out the names of the garrison commander, the aides-de-camp, the ushers, gatekeepers, and bodyguards. You must instruct your spies to ascertain these matters in minute detail.

It is essential to seek out enemy spies who have come to conduct espionage against you and bribe them to serve you. Courteously exhort them and give your instructions, then release them back home. Thus, converted spies are recruited and used. It is through the information brought by the converted spies that native and internal spies can be recruited and employed. It is owing to their information, again, that the doomed spies, armed with false information, can be sent to convey it to the enemy. Lastly, it is by their information that the surviving spies can come back and give information as scheduled. The sovereign must have full knowledge of the activities of the five sorts of spies. And to know these depends upon the converted spies. Therefore, it is mandatory that they be treated with the utmost liberality.

In ancient times, the rise of the Shang Dynasty was due to Yi Zhi, who had served under the Xia. Likewise, the rise of the Zhou Dynasty was due to Lu Ya, who had served under the Yin. Therefore, it is only the enlightened sovereign and the wise general who are able to use the most intelligent people as spies and achieve great results. Spying operations are essential in war; upon them the army relies to make its every move.

*Ralph D. Sawyer translates:

There are no areas in which one does not employ spies.

Practice Counterintelligence—Manager's Commentary

While you get their secrets, protect your own.

You should take deliberate steps to keep competitors from learning what is going on in your business. For example, at one headquarters, a poster in the company cafeteria reminds employees that "loose lips sink ships." The media has run enough stories about corporate espionage to make managers aware of the danger, but constant reminders are needed.

There is evidence that Asian nations readily apply Sun Tzu's lessons on "secret agents." A survey of 1,300 companies conducted by the American Society for Industrial Security revealed that China and Japan head the list of foreign countries possessing the greatest economic-espionage threat. However, next in line were France, Great Britain, and Canada.[3]

When a smaller entrepreneur visited Japan, he found to his surprise that the practice of gathering competitive information is not confined to big companies. After a few drinks one evening, his host took him to a file cabinet and produced a file containing information about the visitor's company.

The first bastion of counterintelligence is usually a memo that requires all employees to refer outside inquiries for information to the public relations officer. This is a good practice since the stories are legion from managers who tell about making a phone call to a targeted company and learning everything they wanted to know.

At the next level of protection are security measures such as a paper shredder in key offices and numbering systems to control key documents like new product plans. Every manager should be concerned about documents on his or her desk in view of visitors because too many people have learned how to read upside down. The best way to handle visitors is to meet them in a separate conference room with no visible company information. At the University of Tennessee football headquarters, the main conference room walls are lined with the ranking of prospective recruits—all covered with opaque pull-down shades.

Security measures are not limited to the office. Although laptop computers are useful on an airline flight, keep in mind that the information may also be useful to a nearby passenger.

The top level of protection is active measures involving checking for bugs in telephones and making sure that rooms engaged for outside conferences are secure and no material is left behind after the meeting.

Part Two

Applying Sun Tzu's Wisdom

The key issue for managers is not knowing
the gems of wisdom from Sun Tzu
but applying the wisdom—
successfully taking action is more
difficult than knowing what to do.

Managers' Examples

Following are useful applications harvested from contributions by managers around the world. Each manager has his or her own favorite quotes. Here are the gems I often consider.

Avoiding Conflict: **To subdue the enemy without fighting is the supreme excellence.** This simple concept of "winning without fighting" differentiates Sun Tzu from the rush to attack so prevalent in Western thinking. His central thesis is to defeat the enemy by using wisdom rather than force. He says, **Subdue the enemy without fighting . . . capture his cities without assaulting them . . . overthrow his state without protracted operations.**

Strategic Planning: **A victorious army wins its victories before seeking battle; an army destined for defeat fights in the hope of winning.** This simple wisdom emphasizes the important role of strategic planning in determining where and how you can win.

Concentration of Resources: **A weak force will eventually fall captive to a stronger one . . .** and **. . . we can keep our forces concentrated while the enemy must be divided.** Statements like these emphasize the value of focusing strengths against weakness.

Achieving Victory: **Use the normal force to engage; use the extraordinary to win.** Too many times plans are for the ordinary instead of the extraordinary. The idea of doing the extraordinary inspired me to display $1 million in one-dollar bills at a trade show to dramatize a million-dollar profit opportunity. We made our point. Sales and profits went off the chart.

Use of Intelligence: **The reason the enlightened sovereign and wise general's achievements exceed those of ordinary men is because of fore-knowledge . . . and . . . know the enemy and know yourself, and you can fight a hundred battles with no danger of defeat.** Good intelligence is as important today as it was 2,500 years ago.

Organizing for Success

John Gledhill
President, Mueller Steam Specialty
St. Pauls, North Carolina

As a new president appointed to turn around a division whose sales and profits were in a slide, I used Sun Tzu's sage advice—***Fight only battles you can win***—to sort through problems of politics, executive turnover, and an outmoded plant. There was a strong temptation to confront the politics and to take hasty, ill-conceived strong measures. We chose not to seek confrontation, but rather to first focus on fixing the plant while learning more about the business.

We followed Sun Tzu's advice: ***Use the normal to engage, the extraordinary to win***. We concentrated our entire energies upon a few small cells within the plant. These small cells, with perhaps 3 percent of the plant's work force, became beta sites where we piloted our concepts and made sure we achieved success. A year later, both beta-site cells have doubled their output. Good associates learned from observing and started to imitate without prodding. The concept of using the extraordinary is also applied when we hold Kaizen events to apply intense focus in small areas with the desire of achieving rapid improvement.

Another key concept from Sun Tzu is: ***Make time your ally***. We have consciously chosen speed and time as metrics for everything we do. In our process improvement activities, we do not spend a lot of time planning. Instead we move rapidly into action and get things done. We have no regrets if we have to tweak things later. We learn more from seeing what works on the shop floor than we ever could in the conference room.

In our business, rapid delivery to the customer is a major consideration. Our old business processes were manual, slow, and batched with execution that too often missed the ship date. The longer it took us to ship an order for standard product, the more calls we received tracking it—further wasting resources.

A long lead time to quote special orders could lose the business. Now we measure how many orders are shipped in 24 hours, how many special quotes our purchasing department can research in less than 8 hours, performance to promise date, etc. Although these are not novel concepts to some, they are to us, and give us the opportunity to make tremendous strides forward.

Sun Tzu's concepts are simple and fundamentally sound. They've helped us be a more profitable producer and a better supplier to our customers. We've made a lot of progress so we won't be pinned down while improving other fronts.

Generating a Winning Strategy

George Schneider
Chairman, La Crosse Footwear
La Crosse, Wisconsin

I found the concepts of Sun Tzu impressive and was equally impressed by examples of how others applied these principles to business. The simplicity of the concepts stimulated my thinking. To energize our organization, I ordered 70 copies of *The Art of War for Managers* and gave them to our sales personnel.

The need for a winning strategy was crystallized by Sun Tzu's statement: *A victorious army wins its victories before seeking battle; an army destined for defeat fights in the hope of winning.*

We understood that for us to have a winning strategy we must follow Sun Tzu's advice to *make an assessment of the outcome.* This focus on the outcome made me look ahead to consider strategies for planning the products we needed to win in the marketplace. Within this assessment, competitive dialogue focused on thinking about the strengths and weaknesses of competitors.

This assessment helped us understand that we must not attack strengths. We decided that we must consider Sun Tzu's advice to *form a single united body at one place.* We found a customer need where we could pit a strength against a competitive weakness. We knew that strengthening our competitive product offering would also strengthen our position in the distribution channel.

This conceptual thinking led us to develop a product we called The Iceman—a unique, well-insulated, rubber-bottom boot that would keep feet warm in cold weather. We tested the boot under harsh cold-weather conditions in the John Bear Grease Sled Dog Race held every winter in northern Minnesota. We used feedback from this event to improve the product and expanded the line to the Ice King, a boot designed for the harshest cold weather.

We featured these unique products in our advertising and again followed Sun Tzu's advice: *Concentrate your forces in the main direction.* We concentrated on media that would reach customers such as ice fishermen, who need extreme cold-weather protection. We achieved a solid impact with our advertising by using the drama of the John Bear Grease Sled Dog Race.

Our reputation for producing high-quality products with outstanding performance characteristics carried through into our introduction of a leather line. This success is important in our diversification to become an all-weather protective footwear source for our customers.

Strategic Assessment Yields Results

William West, VP, Membership Development
Cooperative of American Physicians
Los Angeles, California

Our company provides medical malpractice coverage for physicians in California and competes against companies twice our size. To determine a strategic direction, we used the wisdom of Sun Tzu.

Our industry was in a transition that could best be described as turmoil. Health plans found it easier to purchase services from a few large medical groups rather than hundreds of solo practitioners. Consequently, these solo physicians were consolidating into ever-larger groups.

From these consolidations, new buyers emerged. Decisions once made by physicians were now the responsibility of a corporate buyer who regarded most of the products and services as commodities. As we considered the new reality, we reviewed the time-honored teachings of Sun Tzu: *Know your enemy and know yourself, and in 100 battles you will never be defeated.*

We knew we were a successful growing company guided by physicians who served on our board of directors and committees.

The strongest nucleus of our covered physicians were specialists in neurosurgery, orthopedics, and obstetrics. We developed sophisticated procedures and recruited a qualified staff to deal with the higher risks facing these skilled specialists.

Our competitors, who dominated the primary care practice, were restructuring their plans to serve the corporate buyer whose loyalty went to the lowest bidder. They reduced services to the physician whose reputation was at stake.

As we crystallized our understanding of ourselves and our competitors, we began to gain a better understanding of the battlefield. We turned to a concept from Sun Tzu: *Therefore, to make assessment of the outcomes of a war, one must compare the various conditions of the antagonistic sides in terms of the five constant factors: 1) moral influence, 2) weather, 3) terrain, 4) commander, and 5) doctrine.*

Moral influence was defined by our mission of providing high-quality service to physicians. Our competitors were shifting focus from physician to buyer.

Weather was the external environment that was being disrupted by managed care and reductions in Medicare reimbursements. As a result, physicians' incomes were being reduced, and they were feeling more helpless.

Terrain was the office-based physicians' marketplace that was being consolidated into larger group practices.

Commander was the leadership of our physicians and managers.

As we completed our assessment, we moved away from the herd mentality of marketing to large groups. Instead, we focused on solo and small group practices. This *doctrine* grew from the core principles by which we serve our customers.

We organized around Sun Tzu's concept: ***To subdue the enemy without fighting is the supreme excellence.*** Even though the conventional wisdom in our industry was to focus on serving the large groups, we felt the economic model was flawed. The delivery of health care is the delivery of service by one professional to one customer at a time. Although medical services were being sold "in bulk" to the health plans, no economies of scale were being achieved. Industry experts predicted there would be a fallout, but no one predicted the meltdown that eventually occurred.

We knew that the path toward the objective is not always the most direct route. It is easier to approach 50 group managers than 40,000 doctors. To launch our attack, we retained a consultant who improved our targeting and follow-up. With greater confidence in the effectiveness of direct mail, we doubled our rate of outgoing mail. We invested in specialized training for sales representatives and underwriters. We created new services and discount structures for smaller practices that our competitors offered only to larger accounts. Time after time we found ourselves without opposition in the marketplace. We were truly *achieving victory without fighting.*

Sun Tzu says, *All warfare is based on deception.* Our competition was unaware of the success of our plan. It would be a year before competitors knew what we were doing and another year before they realized the impact. Meanwhile, health plans came under pressure to allow patients to choose their doctors, an advantage for solo physicians. When the choice of a malpractice carrier rests with the doctor instead of a corporate buyer, they frequently choose our services.

Competitors have copied our programs and today are targeting solo and small group physicians. We know this because *we know our enemies as well as we know ourselves.* The *weather* is changing, and we are positioned with strength in the *environment* of a new battlefield. Our *commander* will again apply our *doctrine*, fueled by *moral influence*, and we will succeed.

A Marine Officer's Viewpoint

Bruce M. MacLaren
Colonel, U.S. Marine Corps (Ret.)

Sun Tzu's *The Art of War* has always been close at hand for me, especially during my 30 years as an officer of Marines. In 1953 when I was a cadet at Norwich University, Major General Harmon (Ret.) suggested that all cadets should start reading the Master's treatise as well as Clausewitz. His reasoning was that our nation was becoming more involved in unconventional conflicts. The Korean War focused my attention to General Harmon's suggestion. Later, in 1954, as a new officer in the Marine Corps, my basic training company commander reiterated that all hands should make *The Art of War* required professional reading. In 1963, Brigadier General Samuel B. Griffith U.S.M.C. (Ret.) translated his version of *The Art of War*. He also translated Mao's *Chinese Guerrilla Warfare*.

Both of these treatises became pocket manuals in the field as well as in training during peacetime as far as I was concerned—especially during my many years of service in the Far East. Knowledge of *The Art of War* became a professional link between myself and other foreign officers, especially the Chinese, Korean, Thai, and Vietnamese. I recall many times in Vietnam where our major units would overreact to enemy efforts in the East, only to be struck unaware in the West. Reading Sun Tzu conditioned me to put myself into my enemy's thought process and to better anticipate events. It slowed me down and stimulated my own thought process—let alone probably saving my life.

Even after retirement, I was able to apply the lessons of Sun Tzu in local civic endeavors to keep our town great. Also, as a middle school teacher in social studies, I imparted some of *The Art of War* theories to the best of the brightest who were headed to high school and on to college and corporate endeavors. Michaelson's great book, *Winning the Marketing War,* is still used. The local high school now has its own copy. I must add that Confucius's analysis was better received by some of my less-than-dynamic middle-school students.

Militarily, I favor *The Art of War* translations of General Samuel Griffith, Thomas Cleary, and my old Chinese friend and mentor, Major General Tao Hanzhang P.L.A. (Ret.), whose input helped me earn a degree at the University of Maine. As far as applying *The Art of War* to the business world, Michaelson's work is that of a master! Those who read his advice as they enter the world of competitive business will win their corporate battles; those who don't will fall by the wayside.

Reorganizing the Battlefield

Jay Kurtz
President, KappaWest
Laguna Hills, California

Background: As a student at Canada's Royal Military College, I became familiar with Sun Tzu. As a business consultant, I used the principles of Sun Tzu and other great captains to aid our clients. Here is an example.

Situation: State Bell (not its real name) is a regional telephone company operating in a remote area. The state public utility commission wanted to increase competition and advised State Bell that it expected the company to give up significant market share. New generations of technology were emerging and competition was invading. To satisfy the regulators and incur minimum impact to State Bell, we heeded Sun Tzu's advice: ***Enlightened rulers must deliberate upon the plans to go to battle, and good generals carefully execute them.***

Strategy: Sun Tzu says, ***Wise generals win because they have foreknowledge.*** State Bell undertook a market study and classified customers as:

- Green—would very likely stay with State Bell
- Amber—would not actively seek a competitive system, but would seriously consider another company's proposal
- Red—would aggressively look for a competitor to replace State Bell

State Bell persuaded the utility commission to define the reduction in terms of number of customers instead of number of lines. It then redefined the market using Sun Tzu's advice to ***make use of both the high and low-lying grounds.*** "High ground" was customers with the greater number of lines. The "swamps" were smaller red and amber customers with fewer lines and lower revenue.

Implementation: We organized around Sun Tzu's wisdom: ***By taking into account the favorable factors, he makes his plan feasible.*** State Bell trained a team of sales personnel to convert the larger amber customers with more lines to the newest generation of technology. They also sought longer leases with large customers. In its strategic withdrawal, State Bell allowed competitors to "capture" smaller customers with fewer lines. Consequently, it did not allow any competitor to achieve the critical mass that would justify a full-time service center in any area. This gave State Bell an important service quality superiority.

Results: State Bell lost enough customers—30 percent—to satisfy the utility commission's measure of customers. State Bell won this battle by keeping the bigger customers so that it lost only 15 percent of its lines and revenue.

Florida's Approach: Have Fun in Sun Tzu

Gary Lundy
The Knoxville News-Sentinel
September 18, 1997

If you want to understand Florida football coach Steve Spurrier, you need to read *The Art of War*. Gators center Wylie Ritch said Spurrier handed the players a passage from the book after the opening game this season.

"It was a little sheet that told about a guy teaching these generals how to be leaders," Ritch said. "Four lower-ranking guys went with the four generals trying to help them out. When the generals didn't do what he (Master Sun Tzu) wanted, he chopped off the heads of the guys under the generals. The generals thought, 'Hey, this guy in charge is serious.'"

So the moral of the story is that Florida is going to chop Tennessee's head off Saturday at Florida Field? Wylie laughed. "No, I think coach Spurrier was saying that it was all the coaches' fault we played so poorly in the first game," he said. "He was chopping the assistant coaches' heads off, and his own head off, trying to make us feel bad."

Sun Tzu, huh? I wonder if he wore a visor.

I headed to the nearest bookstore in Gainesville, plunked down $14.95, and proceeded to do some investigative reporting. I soon discovered Sun Tzu wrote an entire chapter on the use of spies.

Page 79: *Having converted spies means getting hold of the enemy's spies and using them for our own purposes.* Remember former UT assistant Jack Sells faxing part of UT's playbook to Ron Zook? Now we know. It all goes back to this dude, Sun Tzu. I couldn't find any mention of Kinko's, though. Guess they didn't have any of those in China in 500 B.C.

Florida Field is already called "The Swamp," but Ben Hill Griffin Stadium needs a nickname. *Orlando Sentinel* sportswriter Chris Harry has an idea that seems to fit best: "The House of the Rising Sun Tzu."

The book explains everything:

- Spurrier sometimes likes to agitate opponents. Yep, here it is on page 25: *If the enemy is taking his ease, harass him.*
- Spurrier's new contract is for about $2 million a year. Page 12: *The expenditure at home and at the front, including entertainment of guests . . . will reach the total of 1,000 ounces of silver per day.* Let's see, at today's going rate of $4.56 per ounce, that works out to about $1.66 million a year for Sun Tzu. Spurrier's package is worth more because he gets far more comp tickets for guests than the general got.
- Florida scored 82 points against Central Michigan and piled up 62 against Tennessee two years ago. Page 20 again: *A clever fighter is one who not only wins, but excels in winning at ease.*
- Spurrier closes the gates to the practice field and is very secretive in UT game week. Page 81: *If a secret piece of news is divulged by a spy before the time is ripe, he must be put to death together with the person to whom the secret was told.* Gulp. "Honest, coach, I won't tell anybody about that double reverse you ran while I was peeking over the fence."

Never did find anything in the book about a visor. However, on page 55 there is a tale about a soldier who picked up a bamboo hat that didn't belong to him. He wore it over his helmet to protect against rain. The commander executed the guy for a breach of discipline.

Moral of the story: UT coach Phil Fulmer shouldn't wear a bamboo hat Saturday afternoon. Especially not if it rains.

Book It: Fulmer Beats Spurrier to the Stacks

Gary Lundy's Follow-up Column
September 23, 1997

At least Phillip Fulmer can say he beat Steve Spurrier at something. He had Sun Tzu's book first. Knoxville's Gerald Michaelson—who helped UT's head coach write *Legacy of Winning*—is one of the world's leading scholars on the ancient Chinese general. The Knox County resident said Monday he gave Fulmer a copy of Sun Tzu's *The Art of War* a couple of years ago.

Sun Tzu's writings are closely studied by Spurrier because the philosophy dating to 500 B.C. relates to football tactics. However, Florida's head coach didn't have a copy of *The Art of War* until last Christmas when a friend gave it to him as a gift.

So if Fulmer had the book first, why didn't he beat the Gators? Hmm, maybe he didn't read it closely enough. Michaelson, who perhaps has the nation's most extensive collection of English language translations of the Chinese philosopher, found this Sun Tzu passage he says may explain UT's 33-20 defeat: *Therefore it is said that one may know how to win, but cannot necessarily do so.*

Wonder if it says anything in there about coaching the offensive line?

Reprinted by permission of the Knoxville News-Sentinel Company.

Timeless Principles

Roger Bean
Coauthor, Powerful Products
Shelbyville, Michigan

Sun Tzu, and most of the other Eastern writings, all confront the East/West barrier in terms of the manner of thinking. What strikes me when reading Sun Tzu's *The Art of War* or Musashi's *Book of Five Rings* is their approach to the problems of strategy. Western thought and approaches to strategy tend to be highly linear and logical. Situations calling for strategy, whether in business or war, involve people, and people do not always act in a linear manner. This applies to Westerners as well as Easterners. Sun Tzu asks the Westerner to think somewhat differently than he or she normally would. The reader finds a new perspective—a more comprehensive and thoughtful view than is typical in much of the strategic literature. This is particularly true of business literature.

Sun Tzu can tend to help one modify his or her mental models, the ingrained mindsets by which we make our decisions. When I want to challenge my mental strategy models (assumptions), I find that the Eastern approaches do that better than many of the less challenging, but more timely, literature. The Chinese were the original "systems thinkers." They did not see everything as being a linear series of polar opposites like good/bad, up/down, courageous/cowardly, right/wrong, etc. By encouraging wisdom rather than rash action, Sun Tzu is decidedly non-Western.

In terms of use, Sun Tzu provides principles—timeless principles. I find I go back and read for inspiration and to get a different and thoughtful look at whatever problem happens to be bothering me. It seldom fails to help when I revisit old and familiar themes, as well as to provoke me to think of new ones. It's a bit like the *I Ching.* Even if you flip coins to get the icons, the *I Ching* provides food for thought.

For me, the ancient military situations spark thoughts that ABC-type business literature does not. It serves the same purpose as: *If looking at it from the right side does not produce any inspiration, then look at it from the opposite side and frequently a thought will occur.* Completely reversing the assumptions or situation often produces results.

So I use *Sun Tzu* to help me think more rigorously. It helps me see things differently. It helps to broaden my mental models. It helps me find the novel or unused path. Like Sun Tzu, "don't fight 'em if you can outsmart 'em."

Win Without Fighting

Jeff Cowell, General Manager
Ingram Fulfillment Services
Ingram Book Group
La Vergne, Tennessee

Some resist the idea of applying military thought to business. I believe this is because people immediately think of battlefield tactics rather than overall military strategy. The marketing how-to books are full of "flanking maneuvers" and "guerrilla techniques." Sun Tzu teaches us to organize our strategy so it is not necessary to fight. (Fighting is destructive, whether conducted on the battlefield or the grocery shelf.) This belief in sound thinking as a way to avoid battle is why Sun Tzu's military strategy can be successfully applied to business.

To win without fighting requires discipline and planning. As a management consultant, I had the opportunity to review numerous strategic plans in a variety of industries. Too often these plans were long on grandiose concept and short on well-planned execution of effective strategies. Often these companies would lurch from one "killer" strategy to another. The consequent depletion of resources would then leave them in the situation so aptly described by Sun Tzu: *An army destined to defeat fights in the hope of winning.* Desperate hopes took such forms as "take market share from McDonald's through aggressive advertising" or "open enough outlets to become the premier distributor of cola-flavored beverages in the U.S."

I would often think of Sun Tzu's advice to focus resources: *If we are able to use many to strike few at the selected place, those we deal with will be in dire straits.* I worked with a manufacturer with a 10 percent market share who faced two dominant competitors with massive economies of scale and extensive distribution networks. Remembering Sun Tzu's advice to concentrate effort, I suggested they focus on the high-end consumer for whom quality and customer service was the overwhelming buying proposition. Using Sun Tzu, they moved from survival mode to a profitable position with lower revenues but much better margins and more cash to the bottom line. By defending the prime territory, they were able to thrive without excessive risk.

The Art of War is a treasure chest of wisdom for leaders who invest the time to understand the text and apply the strategies considering their own experience and circumstances. To meet changing conditions from a position of strength, use Sun Tzu to develop strategies that create a large variety of options. Read and understand Sun Tzu before you need him. If you are on the verge of a great battle against superior forces defending unassailable terrain, it is too late. Remember, win without fighting.

Carving Out a Niche

Larissa Schmidt
Founder, Cyberdesign
Frankfurt, Germany

While waiting at the Singapore Airport for my next plane to Germany, I spent time in the bookstore. I was starting my own Web design business and looked for business literature. Eastern philosophy had always fascinated me so I took a deeper look into *Sun Tzu: The Art of War for Managers* and decided to buy it—a decision I did not regret! As somebody without any experience in the business world, it was amazing to get an insight into this new world. Never before had learning been so interesting and such a pleasure!

Based upon Sun Tzu's principles, I designed the plan for my Web design business. I didn't want to start with something big. To me, it was important to find my "niche," described in Chapter 6 in the section "Gain Relative Superiority." The Internet in Germany is a fast-growing business; a lot of people founded big Internet companies to get a piece of the pie, and a lot of them went bankrupt.

So I decided not to swim with the big sharks in the ocean. I focused on designing home pages for smaller companies, giving them all of my commitment. I decided to let the big Internet companies compete against each other for the big projects. There are a lot of small companies wanting a home page, and they are generally more grateful for results than the big ones!

Another meaningful strategic rule for my business is found in Chapter 12 "Consolidate Your Gains." To do that, you must *develop sustainable loyalty.* Once you have a new customer, it is important to maintain a continuing relationship. This is much more satisfying with smaller companies because a personal relationship is easier to establish. A good relationship with the customer is something very precious. It helps you to identify and satisfy his or her needs. To make a customer happy is the best advertisement you can have because happy customers will recommend you to their customers. In my case, this developed into a chain reaction—my Apple Macintosh distributor recommended me to one of his customers and this new customer now recommends me to her customers.

Finding the book *Sun Tzu: The Art of War for Managers* was like finding a pot of gold. This book helped me to find my way/strategy, set goals for my business, and implement my strategy.

Favorite Applications

John Shamley
Program Director, Compensation
Federal Aviation Administration

When I took my first Chinese history course, I never dreamed I would become a Chinese history major and that Chinese philosophy would be so important to my life. The teachings of Sun Tzu in *The Art of War* are special.

Upon entering the business world, I learned that Sun Tzu had applications I did not recognize as a student. It was particularly relevant to recognize that Sun Tzu's work deals with human beings and their endeavors. Here are a few applications I have found useful.

Be Flexible: My favorite quote is: **Hence no one victory is gained in the same manner as another.** Often in government, we rush to find the "model" or "formula" that makes experience and reasoned judgment unnecessary. What folly! One size does not fit all situations, and we must be flexible in customizing systems to the situation.

Do Not Attack Head-On: **What is difficult is to make a devious route the most direct and to turn disadvantage into advantage.** What Sun Tzu is saying is that we can avoid conflict in solving problems by not using the direct approach. In organizations that did not recognize the need for change, I have seen people "eaten alive" when they tried to initiate change head-on.

Strength against Weakness: **His offensive will be irresistible if he plunges in the enemy's weak points.** In our organization we found the weakness was "intense resistance to change." We recognized that the enemy was us, so we attacked our own weakness and developed innovative and creative responses to change.

Take the Initiative: **A good commander creates a posture releasing an irresistible and overwhelming momentum.** A new compensation initiative had a positive effect on awakening our organizational inertia.

People Are a Valuable Asset: **He treats them as his own beloved sons and they will stand by him until death.** When we treat people as people, the increase in morale and performance cannot be overstated.

Warning: When using the wisdom of Sun Tzu, you will be more successful if you do not overtly state the principles being utilized.

The Importance of Good Intelligence

Brian Stewart
British Diplomat to China (Ret.)
Perthshire, Scotland

I first read the *Bingfa* (*The Art of War*) as an ex-soldier and government servant; relevance to the business world came later. Sun Tzu's insistence on good intelligence is crucial to any serious enterprise—civil or military.

Sun Tzu devoted an entire chapter to the use of intelligence. In his view, knowledge, not only of the enemy but also of oneself, was the key to victory. Every other aspect of Sun Tzu's theories is subordinate to the need for intelligence. Without it, plans are built on sand and guesswork instead of hard fact.

Unfortunately, many people suffer from a serious disinclination to attend to the facts. Either through laziness or arrogance, they adopt the attitude, "Don't confuse me with the facts; my mind is made up." Of all the Sun Tzu principles, his insistence on generous resourcing of intelligence is the one I have always found to be most crucial. In 15 years as a business adviser in China, I found this principle too often ignored by businesspeople. The intelligence failure was not confined to lack of knowledge about the foreign market. These businesspeople knew their own product and the stock market, but knew little about the strengths and weaknesses of their personnel and organization.

Successful penetration of the Chinese market depends on a close study of many factors. We never plunged in without homework and an attempt to identify the Chinese responsible, the availability of budget, and the relevant Chinese regulations. Often I came across companies that had done little or no homework and had not been prepared to spend time or money on a serious study of the market opportunities and problems.

Sun Tzu is as apposite for business as for war. I first came across a copy of the *Bingfa* in the 1970s. I was struck by the fact that although many people had some knowledge of Clausewitz's *Der Krieg* (*On War*) written in the 19th century and possibly of Machiavelli's *Del Arte della*

Guerra (*The Art of War*) written in the 16th century, Sun Tzu's *Bingfa* (*The Art of War*) was hardly known. When comparing all three, I found Machiavelli's views on the importance of intelligence were identical to those of Sun Tzu. Since I could find no record of a translation of *The Art of War* into a European language until the end of the 18th century, I had to abandon the thesis that Marco Polo had brought a copy back with him.

Clausewitz, on the other hand, gave minimal mention to intelligence, and his comments were dismissive; for example, "Most intelligence is false and the effect of fear is to multiply lies and inaccuracies."

Clausewitz, a Prussian staff officer who never had command of an army, still less a victorious one, was plain wrong; and Sun Tzu was right to emphasize the significance of intelligence as an aid to success. A lucky CEO may succeed without doing his or her homework, but the old adage about genius being 99 percent perspiration and only 1 percent inspiration embraces the concept of finding out the facts before deciding on a plan of action.

Sun Tzu said that, if a commander lost the war because he was too stingy to give generous rewards to those who could inform him of the enemy situation, he was unworthy to command. Had Sun Tzu been writing about business, not war, he might have said, "If the CEO has lost the battle because he was not prepared to spend sufficient resources to get intelligence about the market and the competition, he is not worthy to be the CEO."

Sun Tzu's best-known aphorisms on intelligence are: *Know the enemy and know yourself; in 100 battles you will never be in peril* and *when you are ignorant of the enemy, but know yourself, the chances of winning or losing are equal. If ignorant both of your enemy and your-self, you are certain in every battle to be in peril.* Whatever words are used to translate the ancient text, the message is the same: your chances of success are greatly improved if you do homework before committing forces to battle. Of course, the military language must be modified to fit the commercial world. The customer should not be treated as an enemy. Although the customer is a target, he or she is *not* an enemy. The aim should be to make the customer feel he or she is a partner, not merely a buyer or consumer.

Apart from concentration on intelligence to ensure that my clients were addressing the right target, there was another principle to which I adhered: *Never go to war if you can find some other way of proceeding; never go to war unless you are sure you can win; and never fight a battle if you can gain your objective some other way. Wars and battles are costly and to be avoided wherever possible.* As an adviser, it was my duty to make sure that we were on the inside track where there was no competition. If we could not achieve the inside position, there was little point in continuing negotiations since there was unlikely to be a reasonable profit.

Sun Tzu's principles are worth considering in every walk of life, but above all, his insistence on good intelligence and winning without fighting is crucial to any enterprise. In business as in war, ignorance is not bliss and head-on collisions are to be avoided.

Sun Tzu in the Boardroom

Domminick Attanosio
Senior Adviser, Young and Partners LLC
New York, New York

Some years ago I served on the board of a public pharmaceutical company that was developing a new delivery system to provide adjustable dosing of oral medications. The product targeted the pediatric and geriatric markets. I suggested the board consider the following precepts of master Sun Tzu in their deliberations.

Know the enemy and know yourself, and you can fight 100 battles with no danger of defeat. To better know our competitors, we developed a system that monitored the drug industry to track emerging technologies that could impact our dosing system. To ensure our own strength, we engaged the services of the best marketing research and development engineering people we could find.

Travel where there is no enemy. Since the smaller segments of the pediatric and geriatric markets were given limited attention by potential competitors, we guided development efforts into these smaller segments.

Pursue one's strategic designs to overawe the enemy. There were many financial temptations to deviate from our decided mission. We passed by potential investor windfalls in favor of maintaining our long-term objectives.

An army can be raised only when the money is in hand. Authorizing the balance of finances in product development with investor relations, we fulfilled the board's fiduciary responsibility for this emerging public company to assure the timely development of technology with adequate funding for the venture.

The general whose only interest is to protect his people and promote the best interests of his sovereign is the precious jewel of the state. We ensured that our senior managers had proven track records in their respective jobs and adjusted organizational responsibilities accordingly.

The enlightened rulers must deliberate upon the plans to go to battle, and good generals carefully execute them. The statutory responsibility of the board was to keep the company on the offensive with the appropriate management team.

We believed in the philosophy that makes Sun Tzu unique: *To subdue the enemy without fighting is the supreme excellence.* Providing the public with needed technology enabled the board to guide the company to its ultimate victory.

The final chapter in the company's successful history was written when the organization was purchased and stockholders earned an equitable return on their investment.

The Gospel According to Sun Tzu

Joseph J. Romm

Abandoning the traditional, muddling-through, warfare-by-attrition approach, the U.S. fought smarter in the Gulf War. The new military strategy used a theoretical framework developed by the now-retired U.S. Air Force Colonel John Boyd, a pilot in the Korean War. Boyd was puzzled by the fact that the American F-86 sabre jet consistently beat the Soviet-built MiG-15 in aerial dogfights, even though the MiG was a "superior" plane by traditional standards. It could accelerate more rapidly, climb faster, and generally turn tighter than the F-86.

Colonel Boyd discovered that the F-86 had two crucial advantages. First, the jet's glass-domed bubble canopy enabled the pilot to observe enemy activity more easily than did the MiG cockpit. Second, the F-86 could change from one maneuver to another more quickly—decelerating and diving while turning or switching directions. Thus better intelligence and faster maneuver canceled out the superiority of the MiG's. The key to winning, Boyd concluded, was to operate at a faster tempo than our adversaries, to get inside their "time/cycle loop."

How do you develop a system that gets and keeps ahead of the competition? Any organizational system, to be as efficient as possible, must minimize friction. The great 19th-century military strategist, Carl von Clausewitz, said, "Friction . . . is the force that makes the apparently easy so difficult."

In providing the military framework for the new U.S. approach to fighting wars, Colonel Boyd went beyond von Clausewitz's idea of minimizing one's own friction to the idea of maximizing friction for the enemy at the same time. Wrote Boyd, "Mentally we can isolate our adversaries by presenting them with ambiguous, deceptive, or novel situations, as well as by operating at a tempo they can neither make out nor keep up with . . . twisting their mental images so that they can neither appreciate nor cope with what's really going on."

This idea came from Sun Tzu. His book *The Art of War* is a favorite among Japanese businessmen. Sun Tzu's axioms describe an antithesis of attrition warfare. Shortly before the air war against Iraq began, Brigadier General Russell Sutton, director of the Marine Corps operations division, was reported as saying, "The last thing we want to do is to try to meet him [Hussein] head-on. This is pure Sun Tzu."

No Sun Tzu addict, Saddam Hussein relied on forcing us to use direct frontal assaults against fortified positions. We refused to oblige him.

Outline of Key Concepts

Chapter One: Laying Plans

Thoroughly Assess Conditions

Sun Tzu	Business
Moral Influence	Vision and Mission
Weather	Outside Influences
Terrain	Marketplace
Command	Leadership
Doctrine	Core Beliefs

Compare Attributes

- Which side is managed by those who have established meaningful objectives (with a high moral value)?
- Which people have the most ability?
- Which side can take the best advantage of current conditions?
- Which side has better discipline?
- Which side is stronger?

- Which side is better trained?
- Which side is better motivated?

Look for Strategic Turns

- Go beyond ordinary rules.
- Search for advantages.
- Find favorable strategic conditions.
- Examine the situation thoroughly.
- Do the unexpected.
- Build your own strengths.
- Continuously analyze the strengths and weaknesses of the opposition.

Chapter Two: Waging War

Marshal Adequate Resources

When resources are depleted and cannot be replenished, the organization goes bankrupt.

Make Time Your Ally

- Victory is the main objective.
- "While we have heard of stupid haste, we have not yet seen a clever operation that was prolonged."
- When the operation takes too long:
  - Resources may be depleted.
  - Weapons are blunted.
  - Morale is depressed.
  - Your opponents will take advantage of your distress.

- "What is valued is a quick victory, not prolonged operations."
- Those who do not understand the dangers do not understand how to make advantageous use of resources.
- Those who are adept do not require additional resources.

Everyone Must Profit from Victories

- When others go out of business, profit by acquiring their physical and human resources.
- Win by acquiring competitors and making good use of their people in the new organization structure. This is called "winning and becoming stronger."

Know Your Craft

The objective is winning, not spending time. The leaders who truly understand their business control the battle and achieve victory.

Chapter Three: Attack by Stratagem

Win Without Fighting

- Consider making opponents into allies.
- The best victories are those that can be won without conflict:
  - First, attack strategy. This is the best approach.
  - Next, disrupt alliances.
  - If these do not work, consider fighting, but do not attack strengths.

Strength Against Weakness—Always

- The greater your strength compared to your opponent, the greater the chances for winning.
- If resources are equally matched, fight only if you have special abilities.
- The small cannot defeat the large, nor the weak the strong, nor the few the many.

Beware of "High-Level Dumb"

- Those who are not at the scene of action and do not know what is going on should not give orders.
- Each business should be managed by those with extensive experience in that business.
- Rules established at corporate headquarters should not necessarily apply to every distant operation.

Obey Fundamental Principles

- Know when you can be on the offensive and when you must take the defensive.
- Where you have superiority, use one strategy; where you are inferior, use another.
- Seek those actions that have high unity of purpose.
- Be prepared for contingencies.
- Headquarters should be careful of interfering.

Chapter Four: Disposition of Military Strength

Be Invincible

- What you do determines whether you are defeated.
- What your opponent does determines whether you can win.
- Because you know how to win does not mean that you will win.
- Secure your defenses; however, you must take the offensive to win.
- When you have insufficient strength, you must defend.
- When you have an overabundance of strength, attack.
- Tactics used in the defense are different from those used in the attack.

Attain Strategic Superiority

- The best strategy is to win without fighting. This often requires looking beyond the obvious to find the unusual.
- Achieving victory while avoiding conflict requires skillful insight and forethought in planning.
- Your strategy must be so good that:
  - You cannot possibly be defeated.
  - It takes advantage of every opportunity.
- The side that wins will be the side for which victory was certain before the battle began.
- Those destined to defeat fight in the hope of winning.
- The winning leader understands the moral law and strictly adheres to method and discipline.

Use Information to Focus Resources

- Understand your opponent's position and strength.
- Consider where you can have relative superiority.
- Plan to attain overwhelming superiority at a decisive point.
- Build the force of momentum.

Chapter Five: Use of Energy

Build a Sound Organization Structure

- Control is a matter of organization and communications.
- Use the same fundamental principles regardless of size.

Apply Extraordinary Force

- That which directly confronts your opponent is the normal or direct force.
- That which strikes at his or her weakest areas is the extraordinary or indirect force.
- Keep your opponent confused concerning routes of attack.
- Plan the impact of the very strong against the very weak.
- Use the normal force to engage, the extraordinary to win.
- The combination of the normal and the extraordinary is an endless circle of direct and indirect engagements.

Coordinate Momentum and Timing

- Your actions must have the energy of momentum and take place at the most advantageous time.
- Whether there is order amidst apparent confusion depends upon organization.

- When planning creates favorable circumstances, you have the advantage of high morale.
- Whether you are weak or strong depends on all of the arrangements you have made.
- All of the strength will come from the people alone; the leader must create the situation for victory.
- People must be selected for a task on the basis of their ability— not on nepotism or favoritism.
- The energy created is the combined energy of all people and all resources.

Chapter Six: Weakness and Strength

Take the Initiative

- Those who occupy the field of battle first and await their enemy are at ease. Those who come later to the scene and rush into the fight are weary.
- Those skilled in war bring the enemy to the battlefield and are not brought there by their opponent.
- Either offer some advantage to get the enemy to your battlefield or do things to prevent the enemy from coming.

Plan Surprise

Consider these actions to surprise and harass your enemy:

- When at ease, make your opponent weary.
- When well fed, starve your opponent.
- When at rest, make your opponent move.
- Appear where your opponent must hasten.
- Move swiftly where not expected.

Attack	Defense
To take what you attack, attack the unprotected.	To hold what you defend, defend a place that will not be attacked.
Against those skilled in attack, an enemy does not know where to defend.	Against the experts in defense, the enemy does not know where to attack.
Those whose advance is irresistible plunge into their enemy's weak positions.	Those who in withdrawal cannot be pursued move so swiftly they cannot be overtaken.

Gain Relative Superiority

- If I am able to determine my enemy's dispositions while I conceal my own, then:
  - I can concentrate and my enemy must divide.
  - I can use my strength to attack a fraction of my enemy's strength; therefore, I will be superior.
- The enemy must not know where I intend to give battle.
  - If my opponent does not, he or she must prepare in many places.
  - If my opponent prepares in many places, those I fight in any one place will be few.
- One who has few must prepare against the enemy.
- One who has many makes the enemy prepare against him or her.

Seek Knowledge

- Those who know where and when the battle will be fought can marshal all of their resources to the right place.
- If one knows neither where nor when the battle will be fought, his or her forces will be unable to aid each other.

- Victory can be created. (Even if the enemy is more numerous, we can prevent him or her from engaging.)
- Determine the enemy's plans and we know whether our strategy will work.
- Stir the enemy up and determine his or her patterns.
- Probe to learn strengths and weaknesses.

Be Flexible

- While you shape your opponent, do not let him or her discern your shape.
- Strategies do not change with the times.
- Change strategies when they become too obvious.
- Just as water rushes down and shapes its course according to the ground, avoid strengths and strike weaknesses—work out victory in relation to your foe.
- As water has no constant form, there are no constant conditions.
- Because the situation is constantly changing, you must continually modify your tactics.

Chapter Seven: Maneuvering

Maneuver to Gain the Advantage

- Make the devious route the most direct.
- Turn misfortune into advantage.
- Use deception.
- Make changes to confuse your opponent.

Achieve the Critical Mass

- Consider these issues carefully:
  - Know those with whom you enter into alliances.
  - Know the situation and use the help of others who have had the same experience.
- Gather all your resources and you will be too late. Advance without enough resources and you may lose them all.
- Divide the profits of your ventures.

Deceive Your Competitor

The purpose of deception is not to keep your opponent from arriving at the objective; rather, the purpose is to make him or her arrive too late to be of any harm.

Develop Effective Internal Communications

- Have a method for clear communication.
- Do not use the same communications for every situation.

Gain the Mental Advantage

- Preserve your resources for the main effort.
- Do not fight battles you cannot win.
- Adapt quickly to changes in the circumstances.
- Do not do that which your opponent wishes you to do—if for no other reason than he or she so wishes.
- Do not press a desperate opponent too hard.

Chapter Eight: Variation of Tactics

Consider Tactical Options

- Understand the mission, gather resources, and concentrate the offensive.
  - Do not tarry where an advantage cannot be gained.
  - Form alliances where necessary.
  - When limited options are available, resort to strategy.
  - Fight when there is no alternative.
- There are:
  - Business opportunities we should not follow.
  - Competitors we should not attack.
  - Accounts with whom we should not do business.
  - Positions where we cannot win.
  - Instructions we should not follow.
- Advantages alone are not enough.
- Whether at the advantage or the disadvantage, always keep in mind what would be done in the opposite state.
- To gain the advantage, consider what the opponent would do to gain the advantage.
- Use attorneys and others to make trouble for your opponent.

Prepare Adequate Defenses

Do not rely on the opponent not attacking, but rather expect that he or she will and prepare accordingly.

Avoid the Faults of Leadership

- Bravery can lead to recklessness and destruction.
- Being overly cautious leads to cowardice and defeat.
- Anger leads to temper with vulnerability to insults.
- Delicate honor leads to sensitivity and bad reactions.
- Worry leads to oversolicitude and blunders.

Chapter Nine: On the March

Occupy Strong Natural Positions

- Keep close to resources that fortify your strengths.
- Position yourself so that your opponent has a disadvantage.
- Try to keep your opponent from taking advantage of natural strengths that might be available to him or her.

Always Seek the High Ground

- Be concerned for the health of your people.
- Do not occupy imperiled positions; let your opponent do that.
- Fight downhill.

Make an Estimate of the Situation

- Watch for signs that tell you what your opponent is doing.
- Study the actions and mood of your opponent's people.
- If your opponent is giving lavish incentives, he is near the end of his resources.
- Treat every opponent as a threat—be careful not to underestimate.

Discipline Can Build Allegiance

- Treat your people with humanity.
- Instill a sense of discipline.
- Trust and confidence must be mutual—otherwise, it does not exist.

Chapter Ten: Terrain

Know Your Battlefield

- Arrive early and get the best positions.
- In questionable markets, let your competitor enter first to determine whether opportunity exists.
- Develop strengths in narrow niche markets.
- Attack only those segments weakly defended.
- Vigorously defend profitable and unique markets.
- Distant markets can be difficult to serve.

Obey the Laws of Leadership

- If the leader attacks strength, he or she will lose.
- When instructions are clear, everyone will act with confidence; if unclear, every action will be disorganized.
- When leaders are unable to accurately estimate the overall situation, the result will be bankruptcy.

Fight Only the Battles You Can Win

- Use the strength of natural positions.
- Know how to estimate the strength of your opponent.
- Be shrewd in calculating dangers and difficulties.
- It is not enough to know what you should do. You must also put into practice that which you know.
- Do not act in your own self-interest, but rather in the best interests of your people and organization.
- Retreat from bad situations.

Know Yourself; Know Your Opponent

- Knowing yourself is not enough; you must also know where your opponent is strong and where he or she is weak.
- Your chances of victory are greatly enhanced when you attack weakness and avoid strength.

Chapter Eleven: The Nine Varieties of Ground

Choose a Favorable Battleground

Each opportunity must consider the situation:

- Do not fight internally.
- Do not attack or defend where you cannot have the advantage.
- When you can neither advance nor retreat, concentrate on protecting yourself.
- When progress is difficult, keep on the offensive.
- When outnumbered, resort to strategy.
- Fight courageously when desperate.

Shape Your Opponent's Strategy

- Do what you lawfully can to disrupt your opponent's internal communications, cooperation, morale, and cohesion.
- Advance when you can gain an advantage; stay where you are when no advantage can be gained.
- Seize the initiative so you can keep your opponent on the defensive.
- Speed is essential. Move rapidly and miss no opportunity.

Make Victory the Only Option

- The more successful you are, the greater will be the morale and the more certain will be your future success.
- Devise winning plans and actively solicit new resources.
- Make certain the consequences of failure of the organization are understood.
- Fighting for survival assures unity and develops its own strength.
- The skillful tactician accepts the attack in one area and strikes back in another.

Plan Coordinated Efforts

- Foster actions that encourage internal cooperation.
- Do not rely on the physical to win; victory comes only from a tenacious team united in purpose.
- Set high standards for performance.
- Utilize the strength of natural positions.

Press the Attack

- Keep people united.
- Manage calmly.
- Be just and maintain order.
- Understand there are things not to say publicly because this would aid the opponent.
- Keep the opponent confused.
- Make sure that everyone is motivated to succeed and avoid failure.

Learn Winning Ways

- The leader is knowledgeable concerning:
  - The plans of allies and competitors.
  - The fields of conflict.
  - People who can win.
- Always shape your strategy to the situation.

Chapter Twelve: Attack by Fire

Be Disruptive and Intrusive

- Use the most decisive weapons available to attack.
- Disrupt your opponent and intrude into that disruption.
- Be an entrepreneur in developing your offensive.

Consolidate Your Gains

- Reinforce successful efforts and exploit opportunities that arise.
- Encourage and reward the spirit of enterprise.
- Lay plans carefully and take action.

Exercise Restraint

- Attack only when you see an advantage.
- Do not expend energy simply to gratify your own interests.
- Do not attack to satisfy your own anger.
- Losses cannot be recovered.
- Be prudent and do not take rash actions.

Chapter Thirteen: Employment of Secret Agents

Invest in Intelligence Resources

- A major effort requires major resources. Expect opposition from those who are burdened by this.
- Do not ignore the rewards and honors that will help motivate people. Small sums can bring big results.
- Allocate the resources necessary to gain the information you will need.
- The cost of unnecessarily prolonged operations will be much greater than the cost of information that will help to win quickly.

Establish an Active Intelligence System

- Good information is critical to success. This information must come from those who know the situation.
- Beware of those who can only give opinions. This baseless information will mislead.
- Develop a network that can provide information.
- Send out people whose only purpose is to gather information.
- Invite in all who can be a source of information.
- Look for those special people who may have the most information about the situation.

- Get all the information that can be lawfully gleaned from people whom you interview and from those you then employ.

Practice Counterintelligence

- Do not do things that can give information to your opponent.
- Beware the visitor who gratuitously gives you information concerning your opponent. He or she may also be providing information about you to the other side.

Notes

Chapter One

1. Kenichi Ohmae, *The Borderless World* (Harper Business, 1990), pp.73–74.
2. James J. Mapes, "Envision Success," *SUCCESS*, May 1994, p. 14.
3. Tim Carvell, "Prime-Time Player," *Fortune*, March 2, 1998, pp. 134–144.
4. General Bill Creech, *The Five Pillars of TQM* (New York, Plume/Penguin, 1994).

Chapter Two

1. Captain H. M. Johnstone, *The Foundations of Strategy* (London, George Allen & Unwin, 1914).
2. "The 100 Best," *Industry Week*, August 17, 1998, pp. 37–74.
3. Gerald A. Michaelson, *Winning the Marketing War* (Knoxville, Tennessee, Pressmark International, 1987), pp. 80–81.
4. Shawn Tully, "Merrill Lynch Takes Over," *Fortune*, April 27, 1998, pp. 138–144.
5. Samuel B. Griffith, *Sun Tzu The Art of War* (Oxford Press, 1963), p. 76.
6. Eryn Brown, "The Most Admired," *Fortune*, March 1, 1999, pp. 68–73.
7. Eric O'Keefe, "Gannon Luck," *Polo Magazine*, July/August 1998, pp. 65–68.

Chapter Three

1. B. H. Liddell Hart, *Strategy* (New York, Praeger Publishers, 1967), p. 339.
2. Michaelson, *Winning the Marketing War*, pp. 135–136.
3. Norman Dixon, *On the Psychology of Military Incompetence* (London, Jonathan Cape, 1976).
4. Michaelson, *Winning the Marketing War*, p. 30.

Chapter Four

1. David Ogilvy, *Ogilvy on Advertising* (Vintage Books, 1983), p. 47.

2. Chris Mcrae, "Chain of Thought," *Marketing Business*, April 1996, pp. 34–35.
3. Anne Faircloth, "The Best Retailer You've Never Heard Of," *Fortune*, March 16, 1998, pp. 110–112.
4. Ram Charan, "The Rules Have Changed," *Fortune*, March 16, 1998, p. 159.
5. Katrina Brooker, "Papers Lose Tweedy 'Tude, Find Black Ink," *Fortune*, June 6, 1998, pp. 36–40.

Chapter Five

1. Michaelson, *Winning the Marketing War*, p. 13.
2. Gina Imperato, "Harley Shifts Gears," *Fast Company*, 1998.
3. Gerald Sentell, *Creating Change-Capable Cultures* (Knoxville, Tennessee, Pressmark International, 1998), p. 155.
4. "The 100 Best," pp. 37–74.
5. Richard Behar, "Why Subway Is 'The Biggest Problem in Franchising,'" *Fortune*, March 16, 1998, pp. 127–134.

Chapter Six

1. "The 100 Best," p. 64.
2. Howard Schultz, *Pour Your Heart into It* (New York, Hyperion, 1997).
3. Ronald B. Lieber, "Stop Your Whining," *Fortune*, October 13, 1997, pp. SB3–6.
4. Peter Carbonara, "Mervyn's Calls in the SWAT Team," *Fast Company*, April/May 1998, pp. 54–56.
5. Michaelson, *Winning the Marketing War*, p. 94.

Chapter Seven

1. Michaelson, *Winning the Marketing War*, pp. 92–98.
2. Michaelson, *Winning the Marketing War*, p. 5.
3. Colonel G. F. R. Henderson, *The Science of War* (Longmans & Co., 1905), p. 4.
4. Rucci, Kirn, and Quinn, "The Employee-Customer-Profit Chain at Sears," *Harvard Business Review*, January/February 1998, pp. 83–97.

Chapter Eight

1. Matt Goldberg, "Microsoft Knows How to Operate—Fast," *Fast Company*, April/May 1998.
2. Brig. Gen. Robert L. Stewart, "New Technology: Another Way to Get Oats to the Horses?" *Army*, January 1995, pp. 23–27.
3. Donald V. Frites, "Make Your Dealer Your Partners," *Harvard Business Review*, March/April 1996, pp. 84–95.
4. Anna Muoio, "The Truth Is, the Truth Hurts, " *Fast Company*, April/May 1998, p. 93.

Chapter Nine

1. Lesley Hazleton, "Jeff Bezos," *SUCCESS*, July 1998, pp. 58–60.
2. Herman Cain, "Leadership Is Common Sense" (book bonus), *SUCCESS*, January/February 1997, pp. 41–48.

Chapter Ten

1. Michaelson, *Winning the Marketing War*, pp. 124–128.
2. Michaelson, *Winning the Marketing War*, p. 67.

Chapter Eleven

1. Gordon Bethune, *From Worst to First* (John Wiley & Sons, 1998).
2. Steve Casimiro, "The Khakiest Place on Earth," and Jeremy Kahn, "Getting Flush on Plush," *Fortune*, March 30, 1998.
3. Frank Rose, "The Eisner School of Business," *Fortune*, July 6, 1998, pp. 29–30.
4. Bartlett and Ghoshal, *The Individualized Corporation* (Harper Business, 1997).
5. Ardant du Picq, *Battle Studies* (Harrisburg, Pennsylvania, The Military Service Publishing Co., 1958).
6. Eisenhardt, Kahwajy, and Bourgeois, "How Management Teams Can Have a Good Fight," *Harvard Business Review*, July/August 1997, pp. 77–85.

Chapter Twelve

1. Reed Abelson, "A Push from the Top Shatters a Glass Ceiling," *New York Times*, August 22, 1999, pp. 1, 23.
2. Ohmae, *The Borderless World*, p. 28.

Chapter Thirteen

1. Pascale, Millemann, and Gioja, "Changing the Way We Change," *Harvard Business Review*, November/December 1997, pp. 127–139.
2. Michaelson, *Winning the Marketing War*, p. 34.
3. Edward A. Robinson, "China Spies Target Corporate America," *Fortune*, March 30, 1998, pp. 118–122.

Bibliography

von Clausewitz, Carl. *On War,* Princeton, NJ: Princeton University Press, 1976.

Creech, Bill, General. *The Five Pillars of TQM.* New York: Plume/Penguin, 1994.

Dixon, Norman. *On the Psychology of Military Incompetence.* London: Jonathan Cape, 1976.

du Picq, Ardant, Colonel. *Battle Studies.* Harrisburg, Pennsylvania: The Military Science Publishing Co., 1958.

Fuller, J. F. C. *The Conduct of War.* London: Eyre & Spottiswoode, l961.

Fuller, J. F. C. *Generalship: Its Diseases and Their Cure.* Out of print.

Halberstam, David. *The Reckoning.* New York: William Morrow and Company, 1986.

Hart, B. H. Liddell. *Strategy.* New York, Praeger Publishers, 1967.

Hart, B. H. Liddell. *Great Captains Unveiled.* London: Blackwood, 1927.

Henderson, G. F. R., Colonel. *The Science of War.* London: Longmans, Green and Co., 1905.

Johnstone, Henry Melville, Captain. *The Foundations of Strategy.* London: George, Allen & Unwin, 1914.

Kets de Vries, Manfred F. R. *Life and Death in the Executive Fast Lane: Essays on Irrational Organizations and Their Leaders.* San Francisco: Jossey-Bass Publishers, 1995.

Levinson, Harry. *The Exceptional Executive.* Out of print.

Mahan, A. T. *The Influence of Sea Power upon History.* New York: Hill and Wang, 1957.

Mao Tse-tung. *Mao Tse-tung: On Guerrilla War,* 1937. (From Heinl, Jr., Robert Debs. *Dictionary of Military and Naval Quotations.* Annapolis, Maryland: United States Naval Institute, 1966.)

Michaelson, Gerald A. *Winning the Marketing War.* Knoxville, Tennessee: Pressmark International, 1987.

Sentell, Gerald. *Creating Change-Capable Cultures.* Knoxville, Tennessee: Pressmark international, 1998.

Translator's Bibliography

(Includes only books containing a complete translation of *The Art of War* used for research for this book.)

Ames, Roger. *Sun Tzu: The Art of Warfare*. New York: Ballantine Books, 1993. Includes analysis, complete text, and "five hitherto unknown chapters."

Bruya, Brian. *Sun Zi Speaks* (Sun Zi is the Chinese spelling and more clipped phonic of Sun Tzu). New York: Anchor Books, 1966. This book is illustrated by Tsai Chih Chung, with cartoon-like drawings accompanying each sentence.

Chien-sein Ko. *The Art of War by Sun Tzu in Chinese and English*. Publisher unknown, 1973. Out of print.

Clavell, James. *The Art of War Sun Tzu*. New York: Delta by Dell, 1988. Written by a novelist with his interpretations of the ideograms, which lack the combative interpretations of military authors.

Cleary, Thomas. *The Art of War Sun Tzu*. Boston & London: Shamballa, 1988. Original translation plus extensive commentary by 11 interpreters.

Griffith, Samuel B., General. *Sun Tzu The Art of War*. London: Oxford, New York: Oxford Press, 1963. Extensive commentary throughout.

Giles, Lionel. *Sun Tzu on the Art of War*. Singapore: Graham Brash Ltd., 1988. Includes extensive annotations for every sentence.

Hanzhang, Tao, General. *Sun Tzu's Art of War*. New York: Sterling, 1987.

Krause, Donald G. *The Art of War for Executives*. New York: Berkeley, 1995. Lots of interpretive commentary but may not include entire translation.

Phillips, Thomas R., Major. Numerous translations, including *The Art of War*. Westport, Connecticut: Greenwood Press, 1940.

Sadler. *Three Military Classics of China* (including Sun Tzu). Sydney: Australasian Medical, 1944. Probably out of print.

Sawyer, Ralph D. *Sun Tzu Art of War*. Boulder, Colorado: Westview Press, 1994. Original text plus extensive commentary. *The Complete Art of War Sun Tzu, Sun Pin*, 1996.

Tai Mien-leng. *The Art of War*. Publisher unknown. Out of print.

Tang Zi-chang. *Principles of Conflict*. T. C. Press. Out of print.

Wing, R. L. *The Art of Strategy*. New York: Doubleday.

Zhang Huimin. *Sun Zi, The Art of War*. Publisher unknown. Includes extensive text in Asian languages and succinct commentary.

Index

About the Author

Gerald A. Michaelson is author of:

- *Winning the Marketing War: A Field Manual*
- *Building Bridges to Customers*
- *50 Ways to Close a Sale (and Keep the Customer for Life)*

Using the strategic concepts set forth in this book, Michaelson doubled sales volume as a regional manager, district manager, and corporate vice president of Magnavox/Philips.

He served in national offices of the American Marketing Association, as vice president and member of both the board of directors and strategic planning committee. He has been a director of LaCrosse Footwear and marketing advisor to Abt Associates, Cambridge, Massachusetts.

As a management consultant, Michaelson travels throughout Asia and the Americas. A featured speaker at an international symposium on *Sun Tzu's: The Art of War* in Beijing, China, he returned to conduct management seminars utilizing Sun Tzu's strategic concepts for an agency of the Chinese government.

Michaelson's articles have regularly appeared in *Across the Board, Boardroom Reports, Executive Edge, Sales and Marketing Management, SELL!ING, Marketing News,* and *Marketing Communication* in the United States, as well as in *World Executive's Digest and Traveler* in Asia. He writes a weekly column based on his travel experiences for newspapers in the Scripps Howard network.

Michaelson regularly addresses audiences around the world in workshops and seminars on business strategy, marketing, and sales. He applies his extensive knowledge of military strategy coaching executives on strategic management.

Michaelson lives in Knoxville, Tennessee.

Phone: (865) 966-0908

E-mail: suntzu@teammichaelson.com

Web site: *www.teammichaelson.com*